THE ODD CLAUSES

The Odd Clauses

Understanding the Constitution through
Ten of Its Most Curious Provisions

Jay Wexler

BEACON PRESS

BOSTON

Beacon Press
25 Beacon Street
Boston, Massachusetts 02108-2892
www.beacon.org

Beacon Press books
are published under the auspices of
the Unitarian Universalist Association of Congregations.

14 13 12 11   8 7 6 5 4 3 2 1

This book is printed on acid-free paper that meets the uncoated paper
ANSI/NISO specifications for permanence as revised in 1992.

Text design and composition by
Wilsted & Taylor Publishing Services

Library of Congress Cataloging-in-Publication Data

Wexler, Jay.
The odd clauses : understanding the Constitution
through ten of its most curious provisions / Jay Wexler.
p. cm.
Includes bibliographical references and index.
ISBN 978-0-8070-0090-8 (hardback : alk. paper)
1. Constitutional law—United States. I. Title.
KF4550.W465 2011
342.7302—dc22   2011012339

For my father and Mary

Contents

Introduction

The Constitution of the United States contains some of the most powerful and well-known legal provisions in the history of the world. The First Amendment, for example, gives us the right to speak our minds without government interference. The equal protection clause of the Fourteenth Amendment stops the state from discriminating against us because of our race or gender. And the Fourth Amendment, as our television crime dramas continually remind us, prevents the police from searching our homes without a warrant. I would bet that in the past twenty years, several hundred books have been written about these important clauses, and for good reason. This book, however, is not one of them.

Instead, this book will shine a much-deserved light on some of the Constitution's lesser-known clauses—its benchwarmers, its understudies, its unsung heroes, its crazy uncles. To put it another way, if the Constitution were a zoo, and the First, Fourth, and Fourteenth amendments were a lion, a giraffe, and a panda bear, respectively, then this book is about the Constitution's shrews, wombats, and bat-eared foxes. And believe me, if you've never laid eyes on a bat-eared fox before, you are in for a treat.

⌇⌇

The idea for *The Odd Clauses* descended upon me about a decade ago. I was working as a lawyer in a small office in the United States Department of Justice called the Office of Legal Counsel. The OLC, as it's known, is the office that is primarily responsible for advising parts of the executive branch—from the various administrative agencies to the attorney general to the White House itself—on issues of constitutional law. You may recall how the OLC made headlines when (long, *long* after I left) it issued the so-called torture memo to justify some of George W. Bush's more extreme foreign policy strategies. When I was at the office, a lot of our work involved reviewing bills to see if they raised any constitutional problems. Sometimes we provided informal advice to an agency head or White House bigwig. Other times, we would write more formal legal opinions on issues that came up in the day-to-day life of the executive branch: Can the president withhold information about a pardon decision from curious members of Congress? Can the president designate a national monument in the middle of the ocean? When (if ever) can presidents refuse to enforce a law that they genuinely believe is unconstitutional?

Like most lawyers, I had taken my share of constitutional law classes while in law school, which means that, for the most part, I had studied the big-time clauses—the constitutional lions, tigers, and bears. I had taken the obligatory Introduction to Constitutional Law course in my first year and learned about the due process and equal protection clauses. In my second year, I learned about freedom of speech and religion in a course on the First Amendment. The Fourth, Fifth, and Sixth amendments were the topics of a third-year course in criminal procedure. Because I had a special interest in constitutional law and had heard great things about the professor, I also took a course in voting rights, which involved studying a few obscure parts of the Constitution, like the clause in Article IV which says that "the United States shall guarantee to Every State in this Union a Republican Form of Government," but which does not, thank goodness, have anything to do with the Republican Party.

In other words, even though I studied a good deal of constitutional law during my three years in law school, I graduated without knowing anything about most of our founding document. The Constitution, including its twenty-seven amendments, has thousands of words in it, but the well-known parts, even if we generously assume that these include its general provisions establishing the government's three branches, make up only a small percentage of it. The rest of the text is a smorgasbord of clauses that hardly anybody ever talks about in law school, much less anyplace where normal people congregate.

As I quickly learned when I started working at OLC, however, some of these constitutional shrews are incredibly important. Although we worked on plenty of due process and free speech issues, we spent at least as much of our time on parts of the Constitution that I had never run into before. Who knew how much effort an office could exert thinking about the "recommendations clause" of Article II, Section 3—specifically, whether its mandate that the president recommend to members of Congress "such Measures *as he shall judge necessary*" (emphasis mine) renders unconstitutional laws that *require* the president to make policy recommendations to Congress? Who knew how high tensions could flare over the question of what makes someone an "inferior officer" under the "exceptions clause" to Article II's "appointments clause," such that he or she might be appointed by someone other than the president? Part of the reason nobody studies these things in law school is that law professors tend to use judicial decisions to teach the law. For a variety of procedural and other reasons, however, many of the

Constitution's odd clauses—particularly those that allocate power between the branches—never make it to any court. No court means no judicial opinion means nobody in law school thinks about it. But that doesn't mean the clauses do not play extremely significant roles in shaping the nation's constitutional democracy.

It was about a year after I started working at OLC that the idea for the book hit me. I remember the exact day. Bill Clinton was on a trip in Africa, and a village wanted to make him an honorary something or other. The president wondered whether this would violate the "title of nobility clauses," which prohibit officers of the United States from accepting any "office" or "title" from any "King, Prince, or foreign state." The question had to be figured out fairly quickly, so the question came to our office. One of my colleagues was assigned the issue, and in my head I can still see her running around from office to office frantically asking if anyone knew anything about what the title of nobility clauses did and did not prohibit. I had never heard of the title of nobility clauses, so I was no help to my friend. Indeed, I don't recall ever hearing what the answer to the question turned out to be, but I do remember formulating a vague plan that very afternoon to someday write a book about these odd constitutional creatures.

At first, I have to admit, my motivation for pursuing this project was mostly about the cool trivia aspect of learning about the odd clauses. There are title of nobility clauses in the Constitution? How strange! The Supreme Court has original jurisdiction to hold trials in cases where one state sues another state? That's wacky! I still find this trivia fascinating, and I hope you will, too, but as I started focusing more seriously on writing the book, I realized that there are more substantial reasons for studying and writing about the odd clauses.

For one thing, as you will see throughout this book, many of the Constitution's odd clauses raise issues that make front-page news. Maybe you've heard of some of them: Was Hillary Clinton's appointment to be secretary of state unconstitutional because the position got a pay raise while she was still in the Senate? Was it constitutional for Norman Schwarzkopf to accept an honorary knighthood from the queen of England? Could the government use its "marque and reprisal" power to send private ships after Somali pirates? Who owns Ellis Island—New York or New Jersey? Why could George W. Bush appoint a radically conservative judge to an important court without getting Senate approval? Would Barack Obama's plan to tax banker bonuses at 90 percent have violated the Constitution's ban on legislative punishment? And while we're talking about Obama—what's up with the "birther" movement that (crazily) thinks our forty-fourth president was born overseas and is therefore ineligible to serve in the country's highest office?

Even the odd clauses that you don't run across in the papers play a huge role in structuring and limiting our government. Some clauses are so clear, and work so well, that they shape our everyday lives in profound ways without ever calling attention to themselves. They make up, in other words, the background conditions—the constitutional scenery—against which we go about our daily affairs. The Constitution, for instance, says that nobody under thirty-five years of age can become president. This never makes the news, because it's such a part of our culture that nobody ever questions it. But what if the Constitution did not contain such an age requirement? Might Macaulay Culkin have capitalized on the spectacular success of *Home Alone* and run for president back in the early 1990s? The Third Amendment prohibits the army from quartering its troops in private homes in most situations. This seems uncontroversial, but imagine if the clause didn't exist. Might the army try to save money (lots of money) by forcing citizens to open up part of their homes to put up members of the armed forces? Not inconceivable. And horrible to contemplate. Examples like this abound in the Constitution. What if members of Congress *could* routinely be arrested on the way to and from work? What if the government *could* make someone take a religious oath before taking office?

Moreover, who knows when today's odd clause will end up being tomorrow's superstar? Constitutional law is dynamic. It may not always change quickly (though sometimes it does), but it does reliably change over time. Constitutional provisions rise and fall in importance. The First Amendment's "free exercise of religion clause," for instance, was really important for about twenty-five years before the Court took away much of its force in a 1990 case. Just a few years ago, the Court suddenly breathed new life into the Second Amendment when it held that there are limits on how the government may regulate gun ownership. The Court similarly reinvigorated the long-forgotten "privileges and immunities clause" of the Fourteenth Amendment in 1999, when it held that a California statute limiting the welfare benefits of new citizens of the state violated the clause's inherent "right to travel" component. Who knew? Just as a new discovery might catapult a previously unsung animal to the limelight—think here of the armadillo's sudden fame when it was discovered that studying it could give doctors insight into treating leprosy in humans—a change in jurisprudential trends or court personnel might just make today's Third Amendment into tomorrow's, well, Fourth Amendment.

Finally, all the clauses of the Constitution, regardless of their current or future significance, are important for understanding the historical meaning and purpose of the document as a whole. We simply cannot comprehend fully what the framers were up to simply by reading a select few phrases and clauses of the Constitution, some of which (like the First Amendment) didn't even achieve prominence until at least a hundred years after they were written. No matter how odd some of the Constitution's clauses may seem to us now, the fact is that for the framers, *none* of them were odd. Everything had a purpose. Nothing was just thrown in there for fun. If we want to understand the meaning of the Constitution as a whole, then, we need to study all its parts. Just as we can't understand the animal kingdom by studying just a few animals, so too we cannot understand the Constitution (to say nothing of our constitutional democracy that we spend so much time bragging about to the rest of the world) by focusing only on its most prominent features and ignoring its many fascinating odd parts.

But which clauses to write about? The Constitution has a lot of seemingly odd clauses in it, and I didn't want to write an encyclopedia of the entire thing, so I had to winnow the clauses down to some manageable number. I ended up writing about ten, but in the course of thinking about the book, I considered close to twenty. I talked to a lot of people about a lot of clauses and presented the idea to the faculties of several law schools. Inevitably in these discussions, the question of what makes a clause "odd" would come up. It turned out that people had a lot of different theories of "oddness." For some, it's the historically anachronistic clauses—like the one about how slaves would count as three-fifths of a person for determining a state's population (incidentally, this was included to *decrease* the influence of the slaveholding states in the national legislature)—that are particularly odd. For others, the real odd clauses are those where it's hard to understand *why* the framers would have included them. Still others suggested that the truly odd clauses are the ones that deal with relatively insignificant matters (creating post roads, for example) that seem to be beneath the dignity of the Constitution.

In the course of all these discussions, I thought a lot about oddness, and so I figure I should say a few words about what makes me think a clause is "odd." For me, it's the specificity of the clauses I've chosen to discuss that make them so intriguing.

The Constitution performs a set of incredibly important functions in establishing and structuring our democracy. It sets up the three branches of government, allocates powers among them, and keeps the branches separate. It lays out the division of power between the federal government and the states, provides the framework for our international relations, and sets out minimum qualifications for the nation's most important officers. It protects our privacy, our liberty, and our right to be treated by the government as equals.

To perform each of these critical functions, the Constitution uses two types of provisions. Some clauses are broad and exceptionally vague. With these clauses, it is almost impossible to know what they mean without seeing how courts actually apply them in specific cases. These tend to be the lions and tigers of constitutional law, like the First Amendment, which says that "Congress shall make no law . . . abridging the freedom of speech" or parts of Article I, Section 8, where the Constitution grants to the Congress such general powers as "regulat[ing] Commerce . . . among the several states" or making laws which are "necessary and proper" to carry out its functions.

In addition to these liony clauses, however, the framers of the Constitution also included a bunch of extremely narrow bat-eared-fox-like clauses to handle very specific issues and problems that related to their broad goals. Thus, while the Constitution protects equality generally through the Fourteenth Amendment's equal protection clause, it also protects equality through the title of nobility clauses, which prohibit the government from making anybody a duke or duchess. While the Constitution governs our foreign affairs by making the president the commander in chief and giving Congress the authority to declare war, it also authorizes the granting of letters of marque and reprisal to private ships as a way of combating piracy. And while the Constitution allocates power between the federal government and the states through a complicated combination of general clauses, it also, through Section 2 of the Twenty-first Amendment, arguably gives states the authority to make laws governing intoxicating liquors that would otherwise violate a variety of constitutional commands.

It is worth noting one other important thing about these odd clauses. Because the clauses are so narrow, they can be understood fairly quickly without reading hundreds of complicated cases and five legal treatises to get a handle on them. This, in turn, makes these clauses much more convenient for talking and thinking about broad constitutional themes than some of the document's more nebulous clauses. To draw one last analogy to the animal kingdom, then, these odd clauses, in addition to being like shrews and wombats, are also like the drosophila fruit flies of the constitutional kingdom. They are funny little creatures that are uniquely suited to help us understand the larger kingdom of which they are a part. To that end, each of the book's ten chapters introduces one of the Constitution's odd clauses—its history, its stories, its controversies, its possible future—and then links the odd clause to some general principle or function of constitutional law (protecting privacy, separating powers, governing foreign affairs), so that you will come away from the book not *just* with a bunch of cool constitutional trivia, and not *just* with a lot of additional knowledge about some really important specific constitutional provisions, but also with a thorough understanding of our constitutional system generally.

Okay, step inside. The constitutional zoo is now open for business. Please don't feed the animals.

CHAPTER I

The Incompatibility Clause

Separation of Powers

No Person holding any Office under the United States, shall be a Member of either House during his Continuance in Office.

Article I, Section 6

When presidents take office and are looking around to fill their most important posts, they often turn to former members of Congress as possible appointees. This is hardly surprising. Former members of Congress know their way around Washington and can jump right in to help achieve a president's policy goals. In the past few administrations, quite a few prominent former members of Congress have held high government office, from Jack Kemp to Al Gore to Dick Cheney to Hillary Clinton.

But have you ever noticed that nobody is ever both a bigwig official in the administration and an acting member of Congress *at the same time?* Have you ever wondered why that is? It's not because nobody would gain from such an arrangement—presidents would be able to gain support for their programs by promising members of Congress plum positions; members of Congress would gain power and prestige; and the members' constituents would have influence in not one but two branches of the government. It's also not because no country has ever tried such a thing—several Western democracies, including England and Israel, have governments in which members of the legislature also exercise some forms of executive power. And it isn't because nobody has ever proposed such an arrangement in the United States. Many influential thinkers and politicians— from Woodrow Wilson in the nineteenth century to former White House counsel Lloyd Cutler and a bevy of his followers in the twentieth century—have strongly urged that members of Congress be allowed to simultaneously hold office in presidential administrations.

The reason that nobody in the United States is ever both a member of Congress and an official in the executive branch is that the Constitution's "incompatibility clause" flatly prohibits it. Concerned about the abuse and corruption that they saw in seventeenth-century England and in the early American colonies—both the king and the English administrators responsible for the colonies would basically bribe legislators to support their flawed policies with promises of high executive office—the framers of the Constitution made it one of their top priorities to ban dual office-holding. Some of the framers even wanted to ban members of Congress from *ever* becoming executive officers. James Madison, however, thought this went too far and proposed the incompatibility clause in its current form, which is why it was constitutional for Kemp, Gore, Cheney, and other members of Congress to assume top positions in the executive branch once they resigned from their legislative positions.

Well, except maybe for Hillary Clinton as secretary of state, but we'll get to that.

As every American learns in grade school, the structure of the United States' constitutional democracy is distinguished by its *separation of powers*. How exactly, though, does the Constitution create this structure? There is no separation-of-powers clause in the document. Indeed, the Constitution doesn't use the phrase "separation of powers" at all. It doesn't say anything that even remotely resembles "separation of powers." It doesn't say, for example, that "the powers shall remain separate," or "separate the powers shall always be," or "powers, you stay the hell away from each other," or anything of the sort.

To understand the US system of separation of powers, it is critical to recognize that the Constitution—appropriately, given its name—*constitutes* the federal government. In other words, rather than limiting a government that already exists, the document actually creates the federal government out of nothing. Specifically, the first three articles of the Constitution create the three branches of government: Article I creates the Congress and gives it certain enumerated legislative powers (discussed in chapter 2). Article II creates the office of president and gives it the "executive power" (discussed in chapter 3). And Article III creates the federal judicial system and gives it the "judicial power" (discussed in chapter 4). None of the branches possesses any power from any source other than the Constitution. This means that for any branch of government to act, it has to find authorization for that action somewhere in the Constitution.

In addition to doling out powers to each branch, the Constitution sets out the procedures that the federal government must follow when carrying out certain important actions, like appointing top officials or impeaching officials gone bad or passing laws. For many of these actions, the Constitution will give specific roles to more than one branch, so that no single branch can do anything all by itself. Thus, for example, the Constitution gives the president the authority to nominate principal officers like cabinet members or federal judges, but the nominations are subject to Senate confirmation. The Congress can pass bills, but a bill cannot become law until the president signs it (unless a supermajority of both congressional houses overrides the president's veto). The Senate holds a hearing on whether to impeach the president, but the chief justice of the Supreme Court presides over the hearing. The Congress and the president make policy for the government, but the judicial branch can determine if the actions of the other two branches are unconstitutional (this power, that of "judicial review," is not super explicit in the Constitution, but the Supreme Court announced it early on, and it's existed ever since). In each of these cases, one of the three branches has the power to check the action of another branch, thus keeping the power of all three branches in a state of balance. Thus the proverbial "checks and balances," another phrase that does not appear in the Constitution itself.

In addition to checks and balances, however, the notion of separation of powers includes the more abstract idea that, by creating three different branches, each with its own enumerated powers, the Constitution implicitly provides that those specific powers belong primarily, if not exclusively, to the branch to which they are assigned and not to any other branch. So, for instance, as we'll see in greater detail in chapter 3, Article II of the Constitution gives the "executive power" to the president. Presumably, then, only presidents (and those to whom they delegate their power) should be able to exercise this executive power, whatever that power might include. Moreover, presidents could plausibly argue that since the executive power belongs to them and them alone, other branches should not be able to infringe upon their exercise of that power, except if the Constitution explicitly allows for such a check, as for example it does when it gives the Senate the power to veto top presidential appointments.

This might seem straightforward, but in practice it gets messy. Part of the problem is that it's not always clear what actually counts as "legislative power" or "executive power" or "judicial power." If the Environmental Protection Agency makes a rule limiting the amount of sulfur dioxide that light trucks can emit per mile traveled, or the Federal Communications Commission bans celebrities from saying dirty words like "shit" or "shitbag" on television, are those legislative actions or executive ones? If the agency then fines a company or celebrity for breaking its rule, and then rejects an appeal of the fine, is that an executive decision or a judicial one? Yes, the EPA is controlled by the president, and the president appoints the heads of the FCC, but the rules sure seem like the kind of general laws that we expect from legislatures, and deciding appeals sure seems judicial, doesn't it? It should also come as no surprise, given human nature, that the various branches might try to take a little bit of extra power for themselves if they figure they can get away with it. As a result, the federal government is riddled with examples of practices that are arguably inconsistent with the notion of separate powers. For instance: presidents have employed troops for military purposes countless times in the absence of congressional authorization. Congress has passed hundreds of laws dictating that the president can only appoint various high officials if they possess certain qualifications (a PhD in botany, for instance, or a certain political party affiliation). Courts set out rules—like the one from *Miranda v. Arizona* telling the police exactly what they have to tell suspects in custody—that seem almost like legislative ones. Some of these arrangements are at least arguably inconsistent with the kind of government the framers thought they had created.

From time to time, disputes involving these arrangements have made it to the Supreme Court, which unfortunately has not provided a whole lot of clarity about what's constitutional and what isn't. Sometimes—like in the 1926 case of *Myers v. United States,* where the Court held that Congress could not give the Senate the right to veto the president's firing of an executive postmaster—the Court has been strict in policing the branches. Other times, as in the 1988 case of *Morrison v. Olson,* when seven justices approved of a statute creating the position of independent counsel—basically a prosecutor appointed by a special court, who is not controlled by anyone inside the executive branch—the Court has been more lenient. As a result of this lenience, the nation was treated a decade later to Kenneth Starr's $40 million witch hunt of President Bill Clinton. When one of these separation-of-powers cases comes before the Court, it's basically anybody's guess what's going to happen. Most of the time, though, the Court has been willing to tolerate at least some interbranch infringement or intermingling, much to the chagrin of some of the so-called formalists on the bench and elsewhere (Clarence Thomas?) who think that the entire modern federal government is unconstitutional.

Although the framers were vague about a lot of this separation-of-powers stuff, they did fear a couple of practices so much that they decided to explicitly forbid them. Article I, Section 6, of the Constitution contains several of these prohibitions. That section, for example, says that members of the House and Senate may generally not be arrested when going to and from the Congress. It also says that these legislators may "not be questioned in any other place" for any "speech or debate" made in either the House or the Senate. The so-called ineligibility clause (which I'll say more about later) prohibits members of Congress from being appointed to any "civil Office" that was created or had its salary increased during the time the member of Congress was serving as a senator or representative. And then there is the most important of these separation-of-powers-fueled explicit prohibitions—the incompatibility clause of Article I, Section 6, which bars people like Jack Kemp and Lloyd Bentsen and John Ashcroft from remaining members of Congress after ascending to executive office: *No Person holding any Office under the United States, shall be a Member of either House during his Continuance in Office.*

Did we need the incompatibility clause to prevent people from holding offices in both branches at the same time? A strong argument could be made that the Constitution's vague separation-of-powers provisions are themselves sufficient to prohibit dual-office holding, but it is simply impossible to know if the Supreme Court would have seen it that way. In any event, the framers were not willing to take any chances. They had seen the English kings bribe members of Parliament with plum executive positions, turning the legislature of that country into a steaming cesspool of corruption. They had seen the colonial governors do the same thing in the new country, filling the highest seats in the land with "bankrupts, bullies, and blockheads." For most of the framers of the Constitution, the idea that a member of Congress could simultaneously serve as an executive official was so horrifying that they weren't about to leave the possibility up to the vicissitudes of the courts. They decided to outlaw the practice right there in the Constitution itself.

No Person holding any Office under the United States, shall be a Member of either House during his Continuance in Office. The incompatibility clause, then, is a rare example of an explicit constitutional prohibition that was intended to further the framers' vision of a government with separated powers. Later, I will come back to the question of whether a government with separate powers is really a good thing. First, though, a few words about what exactly the incompatibility clause prohibits.

According to the clause, if you are a member of Congress, then you cannot at the same time also be a "Person holding any Office under the United States." Usually, the meaning of this phrase is pretty self-explanatory. Cabinet members, for example, hold offices under the United States. So do federal judges. Many important positions in the executive branch that don't quite make it to cabinet level are also covered by the clause. The undersecretary of agriculture for vegetables would be covered, for example, if there were such a thing. The Supreme Court has said, in other contexts, that "officers" are those government employees who exercise "significant governmental authority" and whose tenure, duties, and salary are set by statute. This covers a lot of top government employees, but not all of them. Your typical line attorney or policy wonk or maintenance worker probably does not "hold an office under the United States." If Senator John Kerry wanted to take a job as a dessert chef in the Department of Transportation's employee cafeteria, for instance, and if his pastry-making skills were good enough to land him the job, nothing in the Constitution would stand in his way.

What about the president, though? Could a senator who wins the presidential election choose to remain a senator even after taking the presidential oath of office? Nobody has ever tried it, but some of the top legal scholars in the country have spent a lot of time arguing about the question. The main instigator of this debate is Seth Barrett Tillman, who is not himself a professor (at the time of this writing) but who has written more journal articles than most law professors will ever write in their lifetimes. Tillman is a master at parsing the precise wording of various odd constitutional clauses and coming up with ingenious and often counterintuitive arguments about their meaning. In a series of articles published in the journals of top law schools, he has compellingly (though by no means conclusively) argued that the president "presides *over*" the executive branch rather than being an officer *in* it, and therefore cannot be described as "holding an office *under* the United States," which is what the incompatibility clause actually says. In response, a leading constitutional scholar named Sai Prakash from the University of Virginia's School of Law has argued that the president "occupies an office under the United States because he occupies an office created under the authority of the United States."

From time to time, the issue of whether someone is an "officer" does find its way to some court. Indeed, the question once made it as far as the highest court in the land. Back in the early 1970s, an association of military reserve officers opposed to the Vietnam War sued more than one hundred members of Congress who were also reservists in the armed forces. The question under the incompatibility clause was whether somebody who held a commission in the military reserves was holding an "office under the United States." The federal trial judge who heard the case held that a reservist position was an office and enjoined the members of Congress from continuing to hold commissions in the reserves. Among other things, the judge thought that, "given the enormous involvement of Congress in matters affecting the military, the potential conflict between an office in the military and an office in Congress is not inconsequential." An appellate court agreed with the trial judge, and then the Supreme Court took the case to resolve the issue.

Despite the importance of the question, however, the Court never answered it. Instead, it dismissed the suit for lack of "standing." The legal doctrine of standing has to do with whether a court thinks a particular plaintiff has suffered a concrete-enough injury to justify letting it bring the action. If this book were about "The Most Depressing Legal Doctrines" instead of "The Odd Clauses," then there might be an entire chapter in here about this "standing" thing. Luckily for you, however, it isn't. Suffice to say that before the Supreme Court will let somebody sue the government, it must be convinced that the plaintiff has experienced a very particular, superspecific, nonabstract, actual injury from the government's actions. In separation-of-powers challenges, where the argument is often just that the government is generally not following the requirements of the Constitution, it can be hard for the plaintiff to satisfy the Court's stringent standing requirements. As the Court put it in the reservist case: "[S]tanding to sue may not be predicated upon an interest of the kind alleged here which is held in common by all members of the public, because of the necessarily abstract nature of the injury all citizens share." Nor was the Court moved by the fact that if these plaintiffs couldn't sue, probably nobody could sue. "The assumption that if respondents have no standing to sue, no one would have standing," the Court empathetically remarked, "is not a reason to find standing." As a result of the Court's stingy standing doctrine, a lot of fundamental separation-of-powers issues remain surprisingly unresolved to this day.

Here's a question that sort of mirrors the old "If a tree falls in the forest and nobody hears the tree fall in the forest, has a tree really fallen in the forest?" bit: If a tree that works for the federal government thinks that something it is about to do is unconstitutional, but knows that no court is likely to ever order it not to do it, maybe because of a really depressing legal doctrine like standing, can the tree go ahead and do it anyway? The answer is no, and not just because trees can't work for the government. Government officials, regardless of what branch they serve in (that's a pun), all take an oath to uphold the Constitution. They are therefore obligated to act consistently with the Constitution's requirements. Of course, an executive official or a member of Congress might knowingly do something unconstitutional and still end up not getting in trouble or being fired because of it, but that doesn't mean the action was any more legal or legitimate than robbing a bank and not getting caught.

It is gratifying that in the United States, both the legislative and executive branches have offices whose duties involve advising members of those branches on whether something they want to do is legal, regardless of what, if anything, a court might have to say about the issue later. In the executive branch, the office that performs this function is the Office of Legal Counsel. Unlike the courts, the OLC writes opinions about separation-of-powers issues all the time. At the beginning of the Obama administration, the office was asked to consider whether Hillary Clinton's appointment to be secretary of state violated the Constitution's separation-of-powers commands. The potential problem with her appointment has to do with the ineligibility clause, mentioned earlier. This clause, which immediately precedes the incompatibility clause in Article 1, Section 6, and is often lumped together with it, says the following: "No Senator or Representative shall, during the Time for which he was elected, be appointed to any civil Office under the Authority of the United States, which shall have been created, or the Emoluments whereof shall have been increased during such time." In other words, no member of Congress can take an office if that office was created, or its salary was increased, while the member was sitting in the legislature. Putting the incompatibility and ineligibility clauses together, then, a member of Congress can never serve as an executive official at the same time that she is also sitting in Congress, and she cannot quit her position in Congress to take an executive office if that office was created, or its salary was increased, while the member had been sitting in Congress.

Well, obviously the position of secretary of state was not created while Hillary Clinton was serving as one of New York's two senators, but the secretary's salary *was* increased by an executive order that President George W. Bush signed in 2008. Doesn't this mean, then, that Hillary Clinton's appointment as secretary of state violated the ineligibility clause, and that she could not legally be appointed to that position until 2013, when her term as senator was set to expire?

It turns out that this conundrum has come up several times in US history, and the executive branch has flip-flopped all over the place about what to do about it. In the beginning, the executive took a strong tack against nominating someone who seemed to violate the ineligibility provision. President Washington, for example, withdrew the nomination of a senator to be a Supreme Court justice when he realized the position had been created while the senator had still been in office. About a hundred years later, Attorney General Benjamin Brewster wrote an opinion explaining that a senator could not be appointed to a tariff commission because the commission had been created before the senator's term had expired (even though the senator had resigned prior to the creation of the office). Brewster recognized that there couldn't have been any real conflict-of-interest problem, given the time of the senator's resignation, but he took what we could call these days a hard-core "textualist" position on the meaning of the ineligibility clause. "I must be controlled exclusively by the positive terms of the provision of the Constitution," the attorney general wrote. "The language is precise and clear, and in my opinion, disables [the ex-senator] from receiving the appointment."

Now let's add a twist. What should happen if, after Congress raises the salary of an office, it then passes a law reducing the salary back to where it was in the first place? Can a member of Congress who was sitting when the salary raise was passed take the office or not? Does the subsequent law reducing the salary back to its original level fix the problem? On the one hand, the salary of the office had been increased while the member was sitting in Congress, but on the other hand, by the time the member takes the office, the salary will be back where it was prior to the increase. It's a hard question, and not just an academic one. Indeed, this precise scenario, which is what happened with Secretary Clinton, has occurred many times over the years. The first time it came up, the question was whether President Richard Nixon could appoint Senator William Saxbe to be his attorney general, even though Congress had increased the AG's salary from $35,000 a year to $60,000 a year while Saxbe was a senator, on the grounds that Congress had subsequently passed a law lowering the AG's salary back to $35,000. Again, it would seem that the rationale for the ineligibility prohibition—to prevent the conflict-of-interest scenario where Congress raises the salary of an office so that a member of Congress can then take the position and buy himself a new Jaguar with the difference—doesn't apply, since after the subsequent legislation there's no money anymore with which to buy a new Jaguar. On the other hand, the ineligibility clause does seem to establish a categorical ban: "No Senator . . . shall be appointed" to any office which has had its salary raised during the senator's term in office.

The problem illustrates a recurring one in constitutional law generally—should constitutional interpretation be *pragmatic,* looking at mushy things like the consequences of interpreting a constitutional provision in a certain way, or should it be purely *textual,* looking just at the language of the document plain and simple? One of the most prominent textualists of all time is Robert Bork, who thinks our society is slouching toward Gomorrah and whose nomination to the Supreme Court was famously rejected by the Senate back in 1987. Weirdly, however, it was Bork who first defended the so-called Saxbe fix back when he was serving as the acting attorney general in 1973, a job that he got because he was the only official in the Nixon Justice Department willing to fire Special Prosecutor Archibald Cox during the Watergate scandal. "The purpose of the constitutional provision," Bork testified at Saxbe's confirmation hearing, "is clearly met if the salary of an office is lowered after having been raised during the Senator's or Representative's term of office."

Subsequent Republican Justice Department officials, however, would be far less loosey-goosey in their constitutional interpretation than Bork. When Lewis Powell retired from the Supreme Court in 1987, one of the top prospects to replace him was Senator Orrin Hatch. The salaries of the justices had been increased while Hatch had been in office, however, so once again the question was raised whether Congress could fix the problem by reducing the salary that Hatch would receive back to its previous level. This time the Justice Department said no. In an OLC opinion written by a superconservative associate attorney general named Charles Cooper (he more recently has defended California's noxious anti–gay marriage constitutional amendment in the courts), the office said that the plain language of the ineligibility clause flat out prohibits any member of Congress from taking any executive office if the salary of that office had been increased during the senator's term in Congress. The rest is history. Reagan appointed Bork instead of Hatch to replace Powell on the Court; Bork's nomination was defeated; Anthony Kennedy ended up on the Court; and now, as the Court's swing vote, Kennedy basically determines the law for the nation all by himself.

So if Orrin Hatch couldn't be a Supreme Court justice, why could Hillary Clinton be named secretary of state? The answer is simple. By the time President Obama got around to nominating Hillary Clinton for the post, liberal pragmatists had taken back the OLC. When Obama asked the Justice Department if a bill reducing the secretary's salary back to its pre-2008 level would make it constitutional to nominate Clinton, OLC issued an opinion that approved of the fix.

Citing the history and purposes of the ineligibility clause, as well as the "practice of the political branches for more than a century," the office concluded that "salary rollbacks achieve compliance with the Ineligibility Clause." The result? Hillary Clinton took office, but with $4,700 less per year than she thought she'd have, which, given the Clintons' legal bills, was nothing to sneeze at.

The incompatibility clause may be fairly obscure to the average American citizen, and even to the average American lawyer, but for a while back in the early to mid-1980s, it was the centerpiece of a high-profile campaign to radically change American government by weakening the US system of separated powers. At least one of the framers of the Constitution thought the clause was the "cornerstone on which our liberties depend," and at least two modern commentators have argued that without the clause, the United States might have developed a parliamentary system of government like the ones that exist in England or France. So it is not surprising that people who do not like separation of powers would target the incompatibility clause. But why would anyone want to take aim at the separation of powers?

The framers insisted on separating governmental powers because they were terrified by the prospect of concentrated authority, which they thought was a prescription for tyranny. After all, they had fled England and fought a revolution to free themselves from the despotism of a corrupt king with seemingly unlimited power. Preoccupied with avoiding concentrated power, the framers broke it up in all sorts of ways—they created the three branches, made two houses rather than one house in the Congress, gave separate roles to the federal government and the states, wrote the First Amendment religion clauses to separate church and state, and used the amendment's speech and press clauses to create an independent press and protect dissent. Their idea was that if the country had all sorts of different centers of power, it would be far less likely that any one of those power centers would be able to impose tyrannical rule on the rest of the nation.

Separating powers comes with costs, however. A system of government with different centers of power is slow and inefficient by design. No one center of power—the president, the Senate, the House, et cetera—can do anything bad all by itself, but no center of power can do anything good all by itself either. The system makes it difficult for government to solve complex problems like the ones that we face every day in our modern society. For example, although I'm sure that by the time you read this our government will have completely solved the nation's enormous health-care crisis once and for all, as I'm writing, the country is in the middle of a fierce debate over whether reform is necessary and, if it is, what kind of reform would be best. The president has one idea; the Senate another; the House yet another. If the president alone could make policy without having to go through Congress, we wouldn't be stuck in this stalemate and we could move on to other things, like solving the country's massive parking problem.

Throughout our history, prominent critics have from time to time complained that the costs of separated government outweigh its benefits. One of the most famous of these critics was Woodrow Wilson, the twenty-eighth president of the United States, who wrote a paper on the topic as an undergraduate at Princeton and then developed his ideas into a book published well before he was elected to office. According to Wilson, a government with separate powers is inevitably both ineffective and unresponsive to the people whom it represents. Wilson thought that if the framers could have seen how the country had evolved by the time he was writing (the 1880s), they would have been "the first to admit that the only fruit of dividing power had been to make it irresponsible." Although Wilson had problems with many of the aspects of the American system of separated powers, he specifically argued in favor of amending the incompatibility clause so that members of Congress could serve in the president's cabinet, something he thought was critical to moving the nation toward the British system that he thought was way better than the American one.

Following in Wilson's footsteps, a group of reformers in the early 1980s took up the cause of challenging the incompatibility clause as part of an overall assault on the system of separated powers. The group was small (maybe around two hundred members) but well-heeled and powerful—it consisted of a senator and a former treasury secretary and other officials and scholars, including Lloyd Cutler, who was a two-time White House counsel and a founding partner of one of the country's most formidable private law firms. The group, which called itself the Committee on the Constitutional System, held meetings and published papers and advocated a complete reformation of our three-branch structure. In a collection of papers entitled *Reforming American Government*, the group provided specific recommendations about how to amend the Constitution to achieve its goals. With regard to the incompatibility clause specifically, the group had this to say:

> The United States is unique among the major democracies of the West in its prohibition of service by legislators in the administration. . . . The prohibition against service by legislators in the executive branch was termed "the cornerstone on which our liberties depend" in debates at the constitutional convention. Little explanation was offered for this judgment, which seems to rest on an exaggerated view of the sep-

aration of powers doctrine and the amount of money a legislator could make in 1789 if he won appointment as a postmaster or customs collector. . . . The proposed amendment removes the existing constitutional prohibition, contained in Article I, Section 6. . . . [T]he change would emphasize cooperation rather than stalemate, and bring a hometown touch to federal agencies now too often isolated in Washington. The proposed amendment might also increase the attraction of a seat in the House of Representatives and thereby work to better the overall quality of the House. In addition, the amendment would somewhat expand the president's choice of executive officials.

The group's book continued with two alternative proposals to amend the incompatibility clause. One of those proposals, for example, would have made it clear that any member of Congress could be appointed to executive office "regardless of the time the office was created or the emoluments whereof were increased, without being required to vacate his or her seat" in Congress. Section 2 of that proposed amendment would have actually required the president to appoint at least four (but no more than twenty-five) members of Congress to executive positions.

Before long, defenders of the US system of separated powers spoke up and vigorously challenged the recommendations of the Committee on the Constitutional System. As a result, the recommendations ended up falling on deaf ears, and the incompatibility clause remained intact. In a way, then, the clause is sort of like a constitutional Utah prairie dog. These small light-brown rodents were brought back from possible extinction (ranchers were poisoning them so they wouldn't eat grass meant for cattle) when the Fish and Wildlife Service put them on the federal list of threatened and endangered species back in the 1970s. Having withstood attacks from their mortal enemies, Utah prairie dogs can now return to dotting the western Utah landscape with furry cuteness, in much the same way that the incompatibility clause will continue to play its critical role in ensuring that the framers' vision of separated government remains the basis of our democratic system.

CHAPTER 2

The Weights and Measures Clause

Legislative Powers

The Congress shall have Power To ... fix the Standard of Weights and Measures.

Article I, Section 8

For us earthlings, no planet is as mysterious and intriguing as our neighbor, the planet Mars. Named for the Roman god of war and known as the Angry Red Planet, Mars calls to mind images of distant colonies, little green men, alien invasions, and involuntary anal probes. Of course, scientists now know that if life ever existed on Mars, it was (or is) probably of the simple, microscopic variety rather than of the three-headed, body-snatching, hobgoblin sort. Still, though, the question of whether life ever existed on Mars remains important, not only for understanding Mars itself, but also for understanding our own planet—where we've come from, and where we might be going.

Accordingly, over the past few decades NASA scientists have spent billions of dollars trying to learn everything they possibly can about our neighboring planet. Among other things, scientists want to understand the current climate on Mars, which apparently holds some clues as to whether conditions on the planet may ever have been hospitable to complex life. Back in the late 1990s, as part of this climate project, NASA sent a $125 million space probe, the Mars climate orbiter, out to gather information and relay it back to Earth. The spacecraft made the ten-month trip from Earth to Mars without incident. As it neared its destination, the orbiter fired its engines in order to slow down and enter into orbit around Mars. At that point, however, something went terribly wrong. The spacecraft was supposed to come out from behind the planet twenty-five minutes after firing its engines, but as NASA scientists nervously waited for it to emerge, no signal from the spacecraft ever returned. The mission was a total disaster. Nobody knows exactly what happened to the orbiter. Some have suggested that it got too close to Mars and either burned up in the atmosphere or crashed into the planet. Another theory has it that the spacecraft remains in space, doomed to orbit around the sun for eternity.

What caused this disaster to happen? In the weeks following the events, NASA scientists studied the data and crunched the numbers. They learned that a key parameter guiding the spaceship's operation near Mars was off by a factor of exactly 4.45. *Aha,* the scientists realized—that's the exact difference between the measure of force known in the metric system as "newton-seconds" and the analogous measure of force in the ridiculous United States–only measuring system known as "pounds-seconds." Officials at the Lockheed Martin Corporation, who built the Mars orbiter, were transmitting this key information in pounds-seconds while NASA was assuming the figures were being sent in newton-seconds. *Oops.* Everybody was in a state of disbelief. How could such a stupid, stupid thing have happened? As one prominent space scientist put it: "This is going to be the cautionary tale that is going to be embedded into introductions to the metric system in elementary school and high school and college physics till the end of time."

The Mars-probe calamity was a substantial setback for the US space program, and American citizens were rightly furious. If we are going to spend hundreds of millions of dollars on space exploration instead of on our roads and schools, then at least we should get things right. Whom should we as citizens hold accountable for the disaster? Clearly, Lockheed Martin bears some responsibility, but as a public agency, NASA deserves a larger share of the blame. What about Secretary of State John Quincy Adams or *Saturday Night Live*'s Dan Aykroyd? As you'll see, both of these guys played some role—however slight—in bringing about the catastrophe. How about Congress? *Congress?* What did *Congress* have to do with screwing up this space mission?

Quite a lot, actually. It is Congress that, under the Constitution, has the authority to decide whether the country should adopt the metric system. If it had done this at some point over the past two hundred years, the Mars-probe incident would likely never have happened. Instead, fearing public disapproval, Congress in the mid-1970s punted the issue to an executive branch agency, which basically did nothing. Thanks a lot, Congress. It turns out that the little bat-eared-fox-like weights and measures clause is a terrific case study for understanding the scope of congressional power and the tendency of modern Congresses to delegate key policymaking authority to administrative agencies, a central and sometimes disturbing feature of American democracy.

In constituting our government, the first thing the Constitution does is to create the Congress and give it powers: *All legislative Powers herein granted shall be vested in a Congress of the United States.* Importantly, the powers given to Congress are not those that are "out there in the world," or those that "one might be able to imagine while tripping," or anything like that, but rather those powers "herein granted." This means that Congress can only exercise the specific powers contained somewhere within the Constitution itself. Congress, in other words, does not have some sort of roving general power to just do whatever it wants.

The Constitution gives Congress a lot of different powers. Working backward through the Constitution, the first place to stop is Section 5 of the Fourteenth Amendment, which gives Congress the power to enforce that amendment's guarantees of equal protection and due process of law against infringement by the states. Congress relied on this power, for instance, when it passed Section 4(e) of the 1965 Voting Rights Act to prevent states from imposing English literacy tests on potential voters. Then there is the so-called property clause of Article IV, Section 3, of the Constitution, which gives Congress the power to "make all needful rules and regulations respecting the territory or other Property belonging to the United States." Nearly one-third of the land in the United States is owned and managed by the federal government, and Congress has used its power under the property clause to carve out from this land our national parks, national forests, wildlife refuges, and all sorts of other designated areas to promote things like endangered wolves, pristine hiking trails, and the clear-cutting of old-growth forests.

Apart from these isolated powers found here and there in the Constitution, however, by far the largest collection of powers is contained in Article I, Section 8. This section is essentially a laundry list of legislative powers. It's kind of a long section, but since it's so important, I thought I'd try to summarize it in the following sentence: Congress may impose taxes, borrow money, regulate commerce, make immigration and bankruptcy rules, coin money, fix the standard of weights and measures, punish counterfeiting, establish post offices, grant copyrights and patents, create lower courts, punish piracy, declare war, create and manage the army and navy, legislate for the District of Columbia, make any law that is "necessary and proper" for carrying out these other powers, and do a few other complicated things that I can't figure out how to summarize.

It might not be immediately apparent, but by far the broadest of Congress's Article I, Section 8, powers is the power to "regulate commerce . . . among the several States." Congress has relied on this "commerce clause" power to justify countless laws over its history, including, for example, most federal criminal laws you can imagine. The commerce clause is also the main source of almost all federal regulatory law, from FDR's New Deal to the environmental movement of the 1970s to the recent (but a little late) wave of financial regulations intended to protect investors from the devious doings of the economic elite.

Although courts used to interpret the commerce clause kind of stingily, these days Congress has wide leeway to enact legislation that has any kind of relationship to interstate commerce. The Endangered Species Act, for example, makes it illegal to "take" any species listed by the secretary of the interior as being endangered. The statute defines "take" as "harass, harm, pursue, hunt, shoot, wound, kill, trap, capture, or collect." It also makes it illegal to attempt to do any of these things, so if you happen to run into a black-footed ferret out on the prairie somewhere, make sure you don't even *try* to harass it. For some endangered species—those which are studied extensively, for example, or which are endangered because some part of them (their fur, their allegedly aphrodisiac body oils) make them targets for poaching—it is reasonably clear why the commerce clause would give Congress the power to protect them. For other species, though, like those cave spiders or tiny toads that live only in a confined area completely within the boundaries of one state, it's not so clear. Why should Congress be able to make it illegal for me to try to harass a spider that lives only in one small cave somewhere in the middle of Texas?

Conservative states' rights advocates have challenged numerous applications of the Endangered Species Act to isolated animals like cave spiders or tiny toads, but so far the lower courts (the Supreme Court has yet to weigh in) have all upheld the statute as justified by Congress's commerce power. The courts have not, however, been consistent in their rationales. Some courts have said that protection of these critters is justified because all species are interrelated in some way, and so saving one species helps ensure that all species, including those that are more directly related to interstate commerce, will flourish. Other courts, however, have relied on the fact that most harms to these isolated creatures come from some kind of real estate development, which is itself clearly related to interstate commerce. As one judge applying this approach put it in a case involving a California toad: "The ESA regulates takings, not toads. . . . The ESA does not purport to tell toads what they may or may not do."

Still, though, even the modern Court has imposed some restrictions on Congress's power to make laws using its commerce-clause power. After about sixty years of letting Congress do whatever it wanted, the Court in a 1995 case called *United States v. Lopez* suddenly cut back on Congress's power under the commerce clause when a slim majority of the justices held that the legislature could not make it illegal for someone to possess a gun within five hundred feet of a school. I remember the day the case came down. I was a first-year law student, and that day my constitutional law professor came into the class and launched into a long diatribe about the decision. The diatribe lasted for maybe five class sessions. Since we hadn't studied the commerce clause at all, none of us had any idea what our professor was talking about, but we did understand that something big had happened. Five years later, the Court made it clear that it wasn't joking around in *Lopez* when it struck down the Violence Against Women Act as being outside Congress's commerce clause power. Since then, the Court has eased up a bit on its commerce-clause smushification project, holding in 2005 that Congress did have the power to enforce controlled-substances laws against local growers of medical marijuana in California, although it's quite possible that this decision reflected the justices' views on smoking weed a lot more than their feelings about the proper limits of congressional power.

Having made this little detour through the Constitution, it is now time to return to Mars and one of Congress's often overlooked powers: *The Congress shall have Power To . . . fix the Standard of Weights and Measures.* Even Congress itself has tended to overlook the weights and measures clause; one prominent constitutional historian has pointed out that the weights and measures power was the very last power that Congress ever exercised. Not that Congress hadn't considered exercising the power quite early on in the history of the Republic; indeed, the question of whether the Congress should fix the standard of weights and measures and, more specifically, whether it should adopt the metric system that the French first adopted in the late eighteenth century, was a question of great importance in early US history. The story of how Congress has dealt with the possibility of adopting the metric system over the course of the past two hundred years is a fascinating one that nicely illustrates some important aspects of the American legislative system, including the critical issue of how citizens should allocate responsibility for policymaking failures among the various branches of the national government.

As early as 1790, President George Washington urged Congress to consider standardizing the nation's weights and measures. Congress, in turn, requested Washington's secretary of state, Thomas Jefferson, to write a report on the matter. Jefferson wrote that report, urging Congress to standardize weights and measures and describing two possible plans, one involving the traditional crazy feet-and-pounds system and the other using the crisp and rational French metric system. A congressional committee apparently recommended adopting the metric system, but nothing ever came of it. In 1816 President James Madison brought the issue up again with Congress, and Congress once again asked the secretary of state to prepare a report. This time the secretary of state was John Quincy Adams. Four years later, Adams submitted his 250-page monster of a report. In excruciating detail, Adams traced the history of weights and measures through the Greeks and the Hebrews, quoted at length from the Prophet Ezekiel, and discussed the effect that the great flood (the one that Noah had to build an ark for) must have had on any preexisting uniformity of weights and measures.

Adams's report was praised to the heavens by some of his contemporaries, but for me, it was damned near impossible to read. In fact, I pretty much gave up when I got to an impenetrable passage about an English law from the year 1266 that purported to describe exactly how many pounds a "farthing loaf" of bread, whatever that is, was supposed to weigh. Anyway, from what I could tell by skimming the rest of the report (and the much more succinct summaries of the report that I could find online), Adams thought it was a good idea to standardize the nation's weights and measures, but he thought it would be a bad idea to adopt the metric system. Among other things, Adams thought it would make no sense to adopt the measurement system of France when most of our commerce was still with England. Not a bad point. In any event, by all accounts, Congress completely ignored Adams's report and did nothing much of importance about weights and measures for another fifty years.

The metric system issue came up again in 1866. In that year, Congress passed a law that made it legal for merchants to use the metric system in the United States and provided that "no contract, or dealing, or pleading in any court, shall be deemed invalid or liable to objection, because the weights or measures expressed or referred to therein are weights or measures of the Metric System." At the same time, the chairman of a House of Representatives committee on uniformity of weights and measures called upon a committee of academics at the State University of New York in Albany to prepare a report on the issue of whether Congress should adopt the metric system as the uniform weights-and-measures system for the nation. This report, much shorter and more accessible than Adams's tome, concluded once again that the United States should keep the zany English pound-and-foot system.

The report rejects the idea of adopting the metric system for a variety of reasons, some pragmatic and others more theoretical. From a pragmatic perspective, the report cites the old "how can we make a change when England hasn't changed" argument, and it also makes a big deal of what a huge pain it would be to convert all the traditional measurements into a newfangled system. The writers further suggest that, given these difficulties, the American people would be unlikely to accept any new system of measurement, particularly one from France: "That the conflict will be fierce in this country, where the people are freer and less habituated to blind obedience to imperial edicts, cannot be doubted," write the authors of the report, "nor will the fact that the system comes from a foreign country, whose language and institutions are alike unknown to us, be without its influence."

The more interesting of the report's arguments are the ones that defend our traditional system as actually being better than the metric system. Better? *Really?* Why? Well, for one thing, the traditional system is better because its basic measurements of length—the foot, the yard, the cubit, the fathom—are all derived one way or another from the human body (the yard, for instance, is described as being "the average distance from the centre of the lips to the extremity of the middle finger, when the arm is extended"—who knew?). Such a system of natural referents, it is suggested, is "more likely to meet the wants of a people than one made amid the turbulence of a revolution, by a committee of learned professors." Moreover, the "short, sharp Saxon words" like "gallon" or "ton" or "bushel" are superior to the long, complicated terms of the metric system, like "demi-decigramme." Indeed, our system is overall much simpler than the alternative, as the authors try to argue by comparing how the two approaches would describe a plot of land: "Every lot of ground 25 feet front, by 100 feet deep, must be described as follows: 7 metres, 6 decimetres, and 2 centimetres front, by 30 metres, 4 decimetres, and 8 centimetres deep. Thus, the description of every such lot will require three different units and six words, instead of one unit and two words." Notice how deceptively absurd it was for the report writers to choose simple numbers from the US system instead of from the metric system; if the lot instead happened to be 30 meters by 10 meters, we would have to say that it was 98 feet and 5.102362204724159 inches by 32 feet and 9.700787401574757 inches. Not so simple anymore, eh? Finally, according to the report, the "base" measurements of the metric system are problematic, either because, like the meter, they are too big, or, like the gram, they are too small, as the authors explain using the example of an absolutely enormous steak dinner: "Hence the weights of all common articles are expressed in very large numbers. For example, a piece of beef, for dinner, which we designate by the modest number, 14 pounds, would have its weight expressed by 6,356 grammes." Oh, heavens! Can you imagine what a nightmare it would be to live in such a world?

The authors also totally unload on the meter. Not only is it too big, but it is also a "fact well known to all men of science" that the meter is "neither a true nor an accepted standard." At the time, the meter was defined by reference to the earth's circumference; specifically, it was defined as being equal to 1/10,000,000 of the distance around the earth of the longitudinal line passing through Barcelona and Dunkirk. Admittedly, that does seem a little more complicated than the average length of a human foot, but the authors of the report go further to criticize the "choice made of the circumference of the meridional or generating ellipse of the terrestrial spheroid, in preference to its axis of revolution," which they contend makes the meter a "sin against geometrical simplicity."

Now, I don't have any idea what any of that means, but I do wonder whether the authors of the report would think differently now that the meter is defined not in terms of the earth's circumference but rather as the distance traveled by light in 1/299,792,458th of a second. My guess is that the change wouldn't have much impressed those grumpy old guys, but apparently the measurement is incredibly precise and stable. Maybe the authors of the report would have turned their ire instead upon the kilogram, which is defined by a platinum-iridium cylinder crafted in 1889 and kept in a chateau outside Paris, where, much to the chagrin of French scientists, it is losing a tiny bit of weight every year.

Skip ahead now approximately one hundred years. In the mid-1960s, England adopted the metric system, thus placing lots of pressure on the United States to do the same. In 1968 Congress authorized the National Bureau of Standards to undertake a three-year study on what should be done about the metric system in the United States. The bureau completed the study, and in a report entitled *A Metric America: A Decision Whose Time Has Come,* urged the country to begin a ten-year conversion process to the new measurement system. Congress didn't quite follow the bureau's advice, however. It passed a law called the Metric Conversion Act of 1975, which came far short of initiating any sort of obligatory conversion to metric. Although Congress recognized that the United States "is the only industrially developed nation which has not established a national policy of committing itself . . . to the metric system," and declared in Section 2 of the act that the "policy of the United States shall be to coordinate and plan the increasing use of the metric system," the law did not mandate that anyone at all had to start using the metric system or even to start thinking about maybe using the metric system anytime in the near future. Instead, Congress created an agency called the United States Metric Board, "to devise and carry out a broad program of planning, coordination, and public education, consistent with other national policy and interests, with the aim of implementing the policy" of the statute.

All Congress did in this law, then, is to delegate consideration of this whole metric thing to a federal agency made up of seventeen presidentially appointed individuals. If you now reread the weights and measures clause ("Congress shall have Power To . . . fix the Standard of Weights and Measures") and then pause to emphasize a couple of times the first word of that clause, you might wonder whether this arrangement is constitutional. After all, the Constitution gives the power to fix the standards of weights and measures to *Congress,* not to some goofy seventeen-member board that Congress creates so that it can avoid having to decide what to do about fixing the standards of weights and measures. What gives?

This question of whether Congress, whose members are elected and therefore accountable to the people, may delegate its constitutional powers to an agency run by unelected appointees is one of the central conundrums of American constitutional law. It is an undeniable fact that most of the laws that govern almost every aspect of our economy come from federal agencies rather than from Congress. Think about environmental law for a second, for example. Sure, Congress has passed some incredibly important legislation to protect the environment—the Clean Water Act and Endangered Species Act come to mind—but who do you think really decides exactly what animals are endangered or how much nickel per gallon of wastewater a plant can discharge into a river? Federal agencies make these decisions, not Congress. And it's the same for all the other agencies that regulate nearly everything we do, from aviation (the Federal Aviation Administration) to labor relations (the National Labor Relations Board) to securities trading (the Securities and Exchange Commission) to food policy (the Department of Agriculture) to a thousand other things. Whether it's because members of Congress don't have the time to deal with lots of specifics, or they feel that an agency full of experts would be more likely to do a good job with them, or they just don't want to take the political heat for unpopular decisions (it's a lot less risky to stand up for endangered species generally than it is to stop a $100 million development project because it might harass a couple of black-footed ferrets), Congress regularly lets the agencies deal with the details of federal law and policy.

A few scholars and other observers think that because the language of Article I gives legislative power to Congress and nobody else, all this delegation of key policymaking power to agencies is simply unconstitutional. Even these critics, however, sort of have to concede that if they're right about Article I, then the entire government as we know it would collapse. Perhaps recognizing this, the Supreme Court has long upheld congressional delegation of power to agencies, so long as Congress provides these agencies with some general "intelligible principle" to follow when the agencies go about their business. Theoretically, this "intelligible principle" test could be quite strict, but in fact the Court has held that almost anything—even Congress's admonition to the Federal Communications Commission to regulate the airwaves "in the public interest"—counts as an intelligible principle. Indeed, the Supreme Court hasn't struck down an act of Congress as violating this rule since 1935. The newly appointed members of the United States Metric Board may not have been particularly powerful, but at least they were constitutionally safe.

So, what exactly did the United States Metric Board do? By all accounts, one thing the members did a lot of was fight with one another. This was almost inevitable, since the Metric Conversion Act that created the board required the president to appoint people representing all sorts of different interests, some (like scientists or educators) in favor of metric conversion, and others (like labor unions and consumers) that were against the idea. This congressional restriction on the president's appointment power is itself constitutionally questionable, but Presidents Ford and Carter went along with it and appointed a lot of people to the board who didn't think much of switching to the metric system. No surprise, then, that the board did not insist on any kind of radical change.

The board did do *some* stuff. It issued publications, aired radio and television public-service announcements, and held town-hall-like meetings to persuade people how great the metric system could be. It urged gas stations to start dispensing gasoline by the liter instead of the gallon, and many stations complied. Other little changes came about at around the same time. Signs on the side of highways, for instance, started showing the distance to upcoming cities in both miles and kilometers (they still do, in some places near the Canadian border). Fifths of liquor—named because the bottle held a fifth of a gallon of liquid—were reformulated to hold 750 milliliters instead (the new bottles held only 0.2 ounces less than the old ones). Consciousness about the metric system among the general public was undoubtedly raised.

For the most part, though, the board did little and was subject to lots of public ridicule. On *Saturday Night Live,* for instance, Dan Aykroyd played a government spokesman explaining the new ten-letter "decabet"—an alphabet made out of only ten letters, including A, B, C, and D ("our most popular letters"); an E-F combo written sort of like a hangman's noose; a smushed-together "GHI" letter; a similarly mashed together "LMNO" letter ("a boon to those who always thought that 'LMNO' was one letter anyway"); and one letter representing all of the so-called trash letters from P through Z. "Ten letters, ten fingers," Aykroyd's bureaucrat explains, beaming into the camera. "Simple, isn't it?" He finishes the skit by working through some examples of how words will be pronounced under the new system ("mucus," for instance, becomes "lmnoucus") and then singing the new version of the now somewhat shorter ABC song.

With a public reception like this, it was no surprise when Ronald Reagan disbanded the board in 1982. The details of the board's demise are interesting. According to a column written by former National Public Radio president Frank Mankiewicz shortly after the death of Ronald Reagan's close assistant Lyn Nofziger in 2006, Mankiewicz had sent Nofziger a column back in 1981 "attacking and satirizing the attempt by some organized do-gooders to inflict the metric system on Americans." This was one position—perhaps the only position—that the conservative Nofziger and the liberal Mankiewicz could agree on, and Mankiewicz reports that Nofziger used the column and other materials the two put together to "prevail on the president to dissolve the commission and make sure that, at least in the Reagan

presidency, there would be no further effort to sell metric."
The two were delighted, but, as Mankiewicz recalls, it was a
"victory . . . which we recognized would have to be shared
only between the two of us, lest public opinion once again
began to head toward metrification."

∽

In September 1982, the poor Metric Board issued its final
report. Among its conclusions? The policy of having two
measuring systems is "confusing to all segments of American society." The perception that metric conversion would be
difficult has "no basis." And there are "no substantial legal
barriers" or "technical problems" with metric conversion.
Nonetheless, thirty years after the board issued those conclusions and then disappeared forever, the United States
remains the only country in the world (with the possible exception of Myanmar) that has not converted to metric.

This is not to say, of course, that we Americans never use
the metric system. Our fifths still contain 750 milliliters of
booze, and our soda comes in two-liter bottles. Illegal drugs
are regularly sold by the gram and kilogram. We run five-
kilometer races and measure the dilated cervixes of women
in labor in centimeters (not generally at the same time). Still,
though, most of our daily measurements remain in the traditional system. Our lumber is sold as two by fours (actually
one and a half inches by three and a half inches), and our
guns (other than the 9mm) are calibrated in inches. Sammy
Hagar has a difficult time driving fifty-five miles an hour.
We measure increasing global temperatures caused by Bush
administration environmental policies in Fahrenheit and
Roger Clemens's steroid-tainted urine in gallons. Al Gore
and I measure our fluctuating weight in pounds and ounces.
Sometimes, we even report the measure of force exercised by
our Mars landers in pounds-seconds.

So let's return now to the question we started with. Whom should we hold accountable for the Mars climate orbiter fiasco? My hunch is that most Americans blamed NASA, but what I've tried to suggest here is that much of the blame—maybe most of it—really should fall on Congress—or, more precisely, all the Congresses that failed to adopt the metric system as our official standard of measurement over the past couple of hundred years. The 1975 Congress that passed the wimpy Metric Conversion Act must get the brunt of the criticism for utterly failing to exercise its constitutional power under the weights and measures clause and creating a wishy-washy agency basically designed to fail to do its dirty work instead. Note that before we can assign Congress any blame for failing to implement some policy, we have to be sure that implementing that policy was in Congress's power in the first place. On the issue of the metric system, that requirement is easily met.

Notice too how the existence of administrative agencies that exercise what rightly might be called legislative power under the Court's lenient "intelligible principle" test complicates the issue of political accountability. Some of the blame for the Mars climate orbiter disaster has to be laid at the feet of the members of the Metric Board itself, for the board clearly had the power to do more to help the country transition to metric. And since the members of the board were appointed by Presidents Ford, Carter, and Reagan and could also be removed and replaced by these presidents, we should remember to include these three leaders on our list of people who deserve some blame for what happened out by the angry red planet.

The Mars probe problem illustrates an issue of immense concern to any country that calls itself a democracy. Critical to the legitimate functioning of any democratic state is the ability of citizens to hold elected officials accountable for their actions. We hold these leaders accountable in all sorts of ways—when we discuss issues with friends, when we evaluate the accomplishments of past leaders, when we speak up on talk radio shows or at town hall meetings, when we write letters and editorials, and, most importantly, when we go to the polls and vote.

When we do these things, we should always remember that Congress is the primary lawmaking body in the United States. It might not always seem that way, since Congress regularly lets executive branch agencies make critical policy decisions. We may be inclined to blame the EPA, for example, when our air becomes dirty, or the FCC, when censors bleep out some celebrity saying "shitbag" on TV, or NASA when our spacecrafts crash into distant planets. And we're right to assign some blame to these bodies, as well as to the president who supervises them and appoints their officials. Ultimately, though, it is Congress that holds the power to make most of our key policy decisions under Article I, Section 8, of the Constitution. As long as what we wish had happened was within Congress's power to make happen, we shouldn't let our legislature off the hook just because some other actor failed to double-check its figures.

CHAPTER 3

The Recess-Appointments Clause

Presidential Powers

> The President shall have Power to fill up all Vacancies
> that may happen during the Recess of the Senate, by
> granting Commissions which shall expire at the End
> of their next Session.
>
> *Article II, Section 2*

When the Supreme Court declared that George W. Bush
had "defeated" Al Gore in the election of 2000, the new
president—lacking anything resembling a mandate from the
American people—vowed to work together with Democrats
to pursue common goals and heal a divided nation. Shockingly, however, when it came to nominating judges to fill
vacancies on the federal judiciary, President Bush did not
always choose moderate candidates who would appeal to
both sides of the political aisle. One of the president's nominees, for instance, was accused of being "racially insensitive"
because, among other things, he had worked to reduce the
sentence of a man who burned a cross on the lawn of an
interracial couple. Another nominee, when asked about
the opinions she had written on the Texas Supreme Court
that she felt proudest about, pointed to such compassion-

ate rulings as those finding against whistleblowers, plaintiffs harmed by faulty breast implants, and children with birth defects.

One of President Bush's most controversial judicial appointments was William H. Pryor, a tough-minded conservative Catholic from Alabama, who Bush nominated to the Eleventh Circuit Court of Appeals (the federal appeals court that decides the law in much of the Southeast) in April of 2003. Pryor, a Republican since the sixth grade and the former attorney general of Alabama, came under fire from Democrats for being hostile to abortion rights, gay rights, and all sorts of other rights. Liberals, for instance, did not like that Pryor had called the Supreme Court's decisions on abortion the "worst abomination of constitutional law in our history" or how he had argued in a legal brief that recognizing a right to gay sex would lead to legalizing sex with animals and dead people. The Constitution provides that government officials like federal judges must be confirmed by the Senate before they can take office. Because of Pryor's radical conservative views, Senate Democrats opposed his appointment and used a congressional procedure known as a filibuster to block his nomination.

President Bush, however, was not deterred. In February of 2004, toward the end of a ten-day break in the Senate's business, Bush used his power under the so-called recess-appointment clause to put Pryor on the Eleventh Circuit without Senate approval. Although presidents of both parties have used the recess-appointment power many times over the course of the country's history, Bush's clear intention to use the power as an end run around the typical appointment process pissed off Senate Democrats. Some, like Senator Ted Kennedy, who filed several briefs in cases challenging Pryor's appointment, were angry enough to challenge Pryor's recess appointment in court. They argued, among other things, that while the Senate may have been (with apologies to the television show *Friends*) "on a break," it was not formally at "recess" when the appointment was made.

Were the senators successful? Did they convince the courts that President Bush's appointment of Pryor violated the recess-appointment clause? Yeah, right, like I'm really going to tell you in the introduction to the chapter.

Much as Article I creates the legislative branch, Article II of the Constitution creates the executive branch. The relevant language in the two articles, however, is a bit different. Whereas Article I gives the "legislative powers herein granted" to the Congress, Article II grants the "executive power" to "a President." The language of Article II gives rise to some esoteric but important issues. For one thing, does the fact that the executive power is given to a president rather than to the "executive branch" mean that the president must have complete control over everything that happens in the executive branch, or can Congress place certain parts of that branch outside direct presidential control, as it has routinely done when creating so-called independent agencies like the Securities and Exchange Commission and the Federal Trade Commission, the heads of which cannot be removed by the president absent actual negligence or malfeasance? Secondly, does the reference to "executive power" instead of something like "the executive powers listed here" mean that the president might possess some powers that are not actually listed in the Constitution but that were generally understood by the framers to be part of something known as executive power back in 1789?

Whatever the answer might be to this latter question, it is widely assumed that the Constitution confers a good number of powers upon the president, some of which are general and vague, and others of which are more specific.

As for general powers, the Constitution makes the president the commander in chief of the armed forces, with the authority to commit and direct troops; the head of state, with the exclusive authority to engage in diplomacy with foreign nations; and the nation's top prosecutor, with authority to ensure that federal law is "faithfully executed." By making the president the head of the executive branch, the Constitution also gives the president the authority to direct the activities of the executive branch through executive orders and proclamations and other memoranda. Recent presidents have used this power, for example, to require agencies to consider the costs and benefits of their regulations, to forbid (or allow) them to do research on embryonic stem cells, and to urge them to install low-flow toilets in their bathrooms to protect the environment.

On the more specific side, the Constitution gives the president the power, for example, to ask for the opinions of his cabinet, to convene the Congress, and to report on the state of the union. More importantly, the Constitution gives the president the power "to grant Reprieves and Pardons for Offenses against the United States." Over the course of US history, presidents have used this power in some really controversial ways, in addition to using it once in a while to free a wrongly convicted poor person. Gerald Ford, of course, pardoned Richard Nixon for whatever crimes Nixon might have committed in office. President Carter used it to pardon Vietnam draft dodgers. And President Clinton left a bad taste in the country's mouth when he pardoned "billionaire financier" Marc Rich right before leaving office.

I have a soft spot in my heart for the pardon power because in my two years at the Office of Legal Counsel, I did quite a lot of work on pardon questions. It might seem like legal issues arising under the pardon clause would be rare, and they are, but they do sometimes come up, and when they do, the stakes are always high. For instance, can a not-so-hot-on-the-death-penalty president grant a death row inmate a reprieve on his execution until the next administration takes over? Does a pardon have to be accepted for it to be valid, or can someone who would like to remain a martyr reject the president's offer? Does granting a pardon require that the president deliver a formal document of some sort to the pardonee, and if so, can the president (or his successor) revoke the pardon before it's actually been delivered? Can the president use the commutation power to move someone from a high-security prison to somewhere less awful, and if so, does that mean (as my boss at OLC once queried) that the president could use the same power to send over a "nice piece of fish" to a prisoner who is sick of eating meatloaf for dinner? Can presidents pardon themselves?

Perhaps the most important power that the Constitution confers upon the president is the power to appoint the government's top officials. The "appointments clause" of Article II, Section 2, says that the president

> shall nominate, and by and with the Advice and Consent of the Senate, shall appoint Ambassadors, other public Ministers and Consuls, Judges of the supreme Court, and all other Officers of the United States, whose Appointments are not herein otherwise provided for, and which shall be established by Law: but the Congress may by Law vest the Appointment of such inferior Officers, as they think proper, in the President alone, in the Courts of Law, or in the Heads of Departments.

What the Constitution is saying here, in its typically crisp and straightforward way, is that the US government has two kinds of officers when it comes to appointments: "principal officers," who must be appointed by the president and confirmed by the Senate; and "inferior officers," whose method of appointment will be set by Congress, which can choose to have them appointed by the president, the courts, or the heads of agencies. One obvious question that arises from the appointments clause is how to distinguish an "inferior" officer from a "principal" one. Another issue is whether Congress can place qualification limits on who the president may nominate. Still another set of questions has to do with what counts as a "court of law" or "head of department." If you find yourself interested in these issues, then I recommend you enroll at the Boston University School of Law and sign up for my Administrative Law Course, where I talk about them endlessly.

The procedure for appointing principal officers—nomination by the president and confirmation by the Senate—works just fine most of the time. If the Senate is in session, it can easily vote to confirm or not confirm the president's nomination to a top post. But what if the Senate is not in session, and the president wants to appoint someone to a very important position in the government? Should the president have to wait until the Senate gets back? The question is important, because the Senate is by no means always in session. Each Congress (e.g., the 103rd Congress, the 97th Congress, etc.) lasts for two years and generally consists of two sessions and one intersession recess. The length of both the sessions and the intersession recess has varied over the years. Prior to the Civil War, the sessions lasted somewhere between three and six months, with the intersession recess lasting between six and nine months. These days, however, the sessions are longer, and the intersession recesses are shorter; the recesses now last somewhere between one and three months. Just as an example, the first session of the 108th Congress ran from January 7, 2003, until December 9 of the same year, and the second session ran from January 20, 2004, through December 8. The intersession recess between the two sessions, then, lasted about six weeks.

Even when the Senate is in session, though, it's not like the senators spend their whole lives together, eating from a communal soup bowl and having pajama parties every night on the floor of the Senate chamber. The senators break for lunch and go home at night and ordinarily have holidays and weekends off. They also enjoy a number of intrasession breaks (I'd call them "recesses" except that whether they deserve to be called "recesses" is kind of the whole problem). In the early days of the Republic, these breaks were rare, but now each session might include anywhere between half a dozen and a dozen breaks, some of which can last a while. During the second session of the 108th Congress, for instance, Congress took nine breaks, most of which were about ten days long, but a couple of them lasted over a month, not much shorter than the intersession recess that divided the first and second sessions of the Congress.

The framers of the Constitution knew that the Senate would not always be in session, and they worried about what might happen to important presidential appointments if the senators who needed to confirm them were back in their home states or vacationing at Niagara Falls or something. Especially because getting from place to place was not nearly as easy as it is these days, when we can just hop on a plane and sit on the runway for six hours before zipping off to our destination, the framers were concerned that the nation might be without a secretary of state or other important official for months at a time. Thus, the recess-appointments clause: *The President shall have Power to fill up all Vacancies that may happen during the Recess of the Senate, by granting Commissions which shall expire at the End of their next Session.* If the Senate is in recess, and the president needs to fill an important post, he can do it without getting Senate confirmation, although the person appointed to the post can only remain in that position until the end of the session after she takes office (unless the Senate comes back and confirms her). The framers thought that the clause was important, but there's no evidence that they thought it would be used particularly often. As Alexander Hamilton wrote in *The Federalist Papers,* the recess-appointments clause was meant "to be nothing more than a supplement to the [appointments clause] for the purpose of establishing an auxiliary method of appointment, in cases to which the general method was inadequate."

The framers might not have envisioned that presidents would use the recess-appointments clause a whole lot, but from the very beginning of the Republic, they have. George Washington appointed John Rutledge to be the chief justice of the Supreme Court by using the recess-appointment power. James Madison used the power to appoint John Quincy Adams, among others, as an envoy to negotiate the peace treaty that ended the War of 1812. Abraham Lincoln used the power hundreds of times, as did Andrew Jackson. Modern presidents, too, have relied heavily on the recess-appointment clause. Ronald Reagan made 243 recess appointments. Bill Clinton made 139, once using the clause to appoint the first openly gay ambassador in the nation's history. George W. Bush used the power to appoint 171 officials, including John Bolton, his unpopular and reportedly insufferable nominee to be ambassador to the United Nations. Bolton, probably one of the only United Nations ambassadors ever to publicly proclaim that "there is no such thing as the United Nations," stepped down from his position in December 2006 when it became clear that the Senate was not going to confirm him.

Some recess appointments are uncontroversial. If the secretary of state were to die on the third day of an intersession recess, and the president felt the need to get a new secretary of state in there before the Senate returned in a month, surely nobody would object. If the same thing happened at the very beginning of a month-long intrasession break, again most likely the president's decision to unilaterally appoint a new secretary wouldn't raise many eyebrows. But what if instead the president wants to make an appointment during a weeklong intrasession break? What if the president wants to wait until the very last day of such a break to make the appointment? The idea that the president has to act immediately because the Senate isn't in session is a complete fiction; the senators will be back tomorrow, or at least by the next week. Moreover, if the president *is* allowed to make a recess appointment at the end of a weeklong intrasession break, why wouldn't it be possible to make a recess appointment after the Senate goes home for the evening, or when it steps out for a coffee break? Can the president really use the recess appointment power in this way? These are some tricky questions, and they bring us back to the case of William H. Pryor.

If there is any office for which the recess-appointment power never needs to be used, it's the office of federal judge. The country is not going to fall apart if some court happens to have a vacancy or two for a month while our senators get some rest and relaxation in the Bahamas. And indeed, although early presidents did use the recess-appointment power to appoint judges, such recess appointments have been rare in modern times. Between 1980 and 2000, for example, not a single federal judge was put on the bench during a Senate recess or break. In recent years, though, as the country has become more bitterly divided politically, fights over federal judicial nominations have become ferocious, with Democrats refusing to confirm Republican nominees and vice versa. So perhaps it is no surprise that presidents, facing a series of

Senate stonewalls, have begun using the recess-appointment power to appoint judges. Clinton put a judge on the federal court of appeals during the Christmas break right before his term ended, and George W. Bush made two such recess appointments—Pryor and the cross-burner-helper guy.

It is also not surprising that these controversial moves have been met with aggressive countertactics, including lawsuits challenging various recess appointments. In the suits challenging Judge Pryor's appointment, challengers made two main arguments. First, they argued that because the position for which Pryor was appointed did not *become vacant* while the Senate was in recess, that vacancy did not *happen* during a recess, and therefore the recess-appointment clause did not give the president the power to appoint someone to fill it. Second, they contended that when the Constitution says "recess," it means only the recess *between* sessions of Congress, and not any little break that happens *during* one of those sessions.

So, what about these arguments? Does the position have to become vacant during the recess for it to have "happened" during the recess? What does the word "happen" mean, anyway? On the one hand, the word does usually mean something like "occur." When we ask when an accident "happened," for instance, we want to know when it occurred. On the other hand, it is plausible to read "happen" as meaning something like "exist," or "be going on," at least some of the time. One commentator points to things like "a vacation, an illness, a sabbatical, a leave of absence, a war," which he says "are generally understood to 'happen' over an extended period of time." "You went to North Dakota for vacation?" we might ask, shocked, upon learning that a colleague had recently spent a week in Bismarck: "When did that happen, and did you at least bring me back a lousy T-shirt?" Okay, fair enough. Still, though, I think the most natural reading of "happen" is more like "occur" then like "exist."

The problem with this reading of "happen" in the context of the recess-appointments clause, however, is that it leads to results that are inconsistent with the purpose of the clause. If we read "happen" in the clause to mean "occur," then the president would not be able to fill a vacancy during a recess if the position had become vacant before the recess, no matter how long the recess was supposed to last. If the secretary of state, for instance, quit or died the day before a two-month break, the president would be stuck with running a government without a replacement until the Senate returned. But the whole point of the recess-appointment clause is to give the president the power to fill important positions when the Senate is not around to confirm them. It shouldn't be surprising, then, that the federal appeals court in the Pryor case joined several other courts which have also held that "happen" basically means "exists" for purposes of the recess-appointments clause, even though that's not the most natural reading of the word.

The intrasession versus intersession issue is harder, in part because neither interpretation is clearly better given the purpose of the recess-appointments clause. Some have argued that because the main purpose of the clause is to allow the president to appoint officials unilaterally during long Senate absences, and because in the nation's early years the Senate's intersession recesses were much longer than its occasional intrasession breaks, therefore the clause should be read only to apply to intersession recesses. The problem, though, is that this length difference disappeared, to a large extent, after the Civil War. Indeed, in the twentieth century, we've had plenty of long intrasession breaks, including at least eight that lasted over a month in the last twenty years, not to mention a two-month Reagan-era break and one in 1948 that lasted over four months. Likewise, we've had some short intersession recesses, including at least one that lasted exactly zero seconds. In 1903, after a single gavel slam ended one

Senate session and began a new one, Teddy Roosevelt appointed 160 officers in what he described as the "constructive" split-second recess that must have existed between the two sessions, an action that the *New York Times* subsequently lambasted, in an editorial entitled "The Infinitesimal Recess," as "preposterous."

What about the text of the clause—does it resolve the issue any better than the purpose? Not really. People who argue that the recess-appointments clause does not apply to intrasession breaks argue that the word "recess" refers to the main break taken during any activity; that the word "the" before "recess" shows that the framers envisioned that only a single recess counted for purposes of the clause; and that short intrasession breaks are referred to elsewhere in the Constitution as "adjournments" rather than "recesses." On this last point, supporters of the intersession-recesses-only argument point to the adjournment clause of Article I, Section 5, which says that "Neither House, during the Session of Congress, shall, without the Consent of the other, adjourn for more than three days."

Those on the intrasession-breaks-count-too side have answers for all of these arguments. They respond that "recess" means any short break (think of a judge telling a jury that there will be a "fifteen-minute recess"); that "the" can refer to a state or condition rather than a single occurrence (as one court put it, quoting a dictionary from 1965, the word "the" can be "used to mark a noun as being used generically" as in "*the dog is a quadruped*"); and that the Constitution makes no neat and clear distinction between "adjournments" and "recesses." For this last point, the intrasession-breaks-count-too crowd likes to point to the pocket-veto clause of Article I, Section 7, which says that if the president fails to either sign or veto a bill within ten days, it becomes a law, "unless the Congress by their adjournment prevent its return, in which case it shall not be a law." Since everybody who has ever thought about it for more than two seconds has concluded that the word "adjournment" in this clause must include the intersession recess as well as any intrasession breaks, the argument follows that the terms "adjourn" and "recess" are overlapping terms in the Constitution.

Because the text and purpose of the clause do not resolve the issue, it is no surprise that the executive branch has wavered in how it has interpreted "recess" over the years. In 1901 Attorney General Philander Knox issued an opinion concluding that the president could not make a recess appointment during an intrasession break, finding it "irresistible" that the word "recess" meant "the period after the final adjournment of Congress for the session, and before the next session begins." But then twenty years later, Attorney General Harry Daugherty wrote an opinion saying that the president can make an intrasession-recess appointment whenever, "in a practical sense," the Senate is on a long enough break that its consent cannot be obtained. While Daugherty didn't say exactly how long such a break had to be, he did make it clear that a really short break like two or three or maybe even ten days wouldn't count. For the next sixty or so years, presidents following this advice made a number of intrasession appointments, but almost never during breaks of less than a month. Then, in a brief filed in 1993, the Justice Department changed course once again and said that the president can make a recess appointment during any Senate break, no matter how short. Subsequently, Presidents Clinton and Bush made lots of recess appointments during extremely short breaks, often within only six days of the Senate's return to business.

As it turned out, the court of appeals in the Pryor case found the government's arguments more persuasive, and Judge Pryor got to stay in office. In June of 2005, more than two years after President Bush first put him on the bench, the full Senate confirmed Judge Pryor to a lifetime appoint-

ment. Three years later, Pryor wrote the majority opinion in
Pelphrey v. Cobb County, a 2–1 decision holding that it was
okay for public commissions to start their meetings by pray-
ing to specific religious figures like Jesus and Mohammed.

⁓

At least at this point in our nation's history, then, the president can make a recess appointment either between the sessions of the Senate or when the Senate takes a break during a
session. What if the Senate doesn't like the president's recess
appointment though? Is there anything it can do to punish
the president or to deter the president from making another
controversial recess appointment?

Enter once again Seth Barrett Tillman, the scholar who
suggested, back in chapter 1, that a senator could remain in
the Senate even after ascending to the office of president. In
a recent article, Tillman suggests that although most people have assumed that the Senate is stuck with the recess
appointee until the natural end of its next session, in fact
nothing in the Constitution prevents the Senate from getting rid of a recess appointee by reconvening, immediately
adjourning its session, and then starting a new session. Or,
alternatively, if the recess appointment in question occurred
during an intrasession break, the Senate could reconvene, adjourn its session, begin a new session, adjourn that session,
and then start a new session, all with a couple of swings of
the gavel. In support of his so-called Tillman Adjournment,
Tillman argues that the procedure would give the president
an incentive to make recess appointments who are amenable
to the Senate and would ensure that the Senate remains accountable to the people by giving it an active role in deciding
whether to keep the president's recess appointments.

Tillman's proposal occasioned a response from Brian
Kalt, a Michigan State University professor who is one of

the country's preeminent experts on the Constitution's odd clauses. A few years back, Professor Kalt gained some much-deserved fame for a brilliant article in which he pointed out that as a result of the interaction between a couple of constitutional provisions and a weird statute, there's a tiny area of land in the Idaho portion of Yellowstone National Park where the government cannot constitutionally prosecute anyone for committing a crime (note to those who would like to try to harass a black-footed ferret: this may be the place for you). Kalt raises a number of legal and practical concerns with Tillman's proposal, pointing out, for instance, that there are much easier ways for the Senate to deal with an overreaching president, including using its power over government money to refuse to pay the salary of questionable recess appointments, something the Senate has in fact already done.

Kalt also argues that if the Senate did what Tillman suggests, the president would fight back. Specifically, Kalt says that the president could reappoint his recess appointments in the constructive recess between the Senate's constructive adjournment and constructive reconvening, and then use his authority under Article II, Section 3, to convene an extraordinary session of the Senate which only the president could adjourn, thus ensuring that his recess appointments would remain in office until he decided to adjourn his special session. I presume that if the president tried such a maneuver, the Senate might respond by saying that it had constructively reconvened before the president had a chance to convene his special session and that therefore his special session never really existed. If this happened, I have no idea what would take place next. Perhaps someone would bring a lawsuit, and an irate Supreme Court would send both the president and the Senate to bed without supper. This, of course, is all quite absurd, but it's in fact not too different from the kind of standoff that occurred at the end of the Bush administration, when Senate Majority Leader Harry Reid kept the Senate in pretty much continuous pro forma session to keep Bush from making any more recess appointments.

∽

When we as citizens think about how the Constitution should be interpreted, usually it's in the context of some highly emotionally charged issue on which we already have very strong feelings. It is inevitable that our views on the underlying issue will affect how we think the Constitution should be interpreted. It is hard, for example, to think dispassionately about the proper method of constitutional interpretation when abortion rights or affirmative action or religious freedom are at stake. I would guess that most people who strongly believe that the government should not interfere with the reproductive choices of women are also inclined to argue that the Constitution prohibits the government from making abortion illegal. But there is a big difference between a policy conclusion that the government *shouldn't* do something and a constitutional conclusion that the government *can't* do something, and it is important to keep these two inquiries separate when thinking about what principles courts should use to interpret the Constitution. After all, principles of constitutional interpretation apply to all cases, not just the one you're thinking about, and if you conclude that the Supreme Court should read text like the due process clause (no state may "deprive any person of life, liberty, or property, without due process of law") very broadly to stop the government from prohibiting abortion, then in the next case some judge who doesn't share your policy views might use your "read the text broadly" principle to conclude that the takings clause of the Fifth Amendment (no state shall "take private property" without "just compensation") prohibits the government from passing environmental legislation that will interfere with the rights of private property owners.

It makes sense, then, when starting to think about how the Constitution should be interpreted, to do so in the context of some part of the Constitution that does not raise your blood pressure too much. A few years ago, a professor at the Cardozo School of Law in New York City named Michael Herz wrote a terrific article that deserves to be read by more than the fourteen people in legal academia who probably read it, in which he suggests that the recess-appointments clause is a great clause to use to think about how the Constitution should be interpreted. Why? Herz explains:

> There are stakes, but they are not too high; there is substantial text to work with, but no shortage of interpretive issues. In considering the scope of the clause, moreover, one is perforce behind a sort of Rawlsian veil of ignorance. A given interpretation may be good for your team at one point in history and bad at another. Therefore, ideology and the appeal of desired outcomes in the short-term can more easily be set aside here than when considering many substantive constitutional issues.

Now, although the word "perforce" is a little too fourteenth century for my taste, Herz's point remains a solid one. Since sometimes the president will be liberal and sometimes the president will be a Republican, your interpretation of the recess-appointment clause is unlikely to be swayed by your policy or political leanings. What's good for George W. Bush one year is good for Barack Obama a few years later. So, when I was talking earlier about the various interpretive problems with the clause, what did you think? On the "happen" issue, where the text of the clause and its purpose seemed to be at odds, which one did you think should trump? On the intersession versus intrasession issue, did you think the Court should read the clause broadly to cover all breaks, or narrowly to cover just the intersession recess? Did you think it should matter that over time, the Senate has changed its practices to shorten the intersession recess and hold more intrasession breaks, or did you think that the original intention of the framers should control regardless of what happened two hundred years later? These are all incredibly important issues of constitutional interpretation that determine the very nature of political and social life in our country. Thinking about them in connection with a shrew like the recess-appointment clause can help us keep our heads straight when later on we find ourselves confronting affirmative action, abortion, or some other constitutional grizzly bear.

CHAPTER 4

The Original-Jurisdiction Clause

Judicial Powers

In all Cases affecting Ambassadors, other public Ministers and Consuls, and those in which a State shall be Party, the supreme Court shall have original Jurisdiction.

Article III, Section 2

Between 1892, when the immigration depot at Ellis Island opened, and 1954, when it closed, millions of people entered the United States through its doors. Most likely, just about all of these new arrivals assumed they had landed in the state of New York. After all, steamships bound for the island listed their destination as "New York." Certificates of Arrival were marked "Ellis Island, New York." And the card pinned to each disembarking passenger read, "When landing at New York this card is to be pinned to the coat or dress of the passenger in a prominent position" in eight different languages. In light of all this, the new residents of the United States could likely be forgiven for not realizing that they may have in fact landed in (gasp!) New Jersey.

Not that New York would have admitted anything of the sort. Indeed, New York and New Jersey had disagreed about the ownership of Ellis Island ever since the Duke of York granted some ambiguous portion of his territory to the proprietors of New Jersey back in the late seventeenth century. The two states entered a legally binding compact in 1834 that set the boundary between the states at the middle of the Hudson River, although the agreement also provided that New York would retain "its present jurisdiction" over Ellis Island, which lies on the New Jersey side of that river. At the time, however, Ellis Island was a tiny pile of mud and oyster shells, and so nobody cared that much.

Although New York and New Jersey would argue endlessly over the years about which one of them owned Ellis Island, it was the national government that did almost everything of note there. For many years, the feds, to whom New York had temporarily ceded jurisdiction over the island back in 1800, used the place as a fortress. In the mid-nineteenth century, though, when Congress decided that immigrants should enter the country on an island due to their "frauds, robbery, and general crookedness," the federal government picked Ellis Island as the nation's new immigration station. Unfortunately, the island was too small for this purpose. As a result, during the forty years following its initial designation as the nation's immigration capital, the federal government used rocks and sticks and other fill material to add over twenty-four acres to the original three-acre island.

New York and New Jersey agreed that the 1834 compact gave New York ownership of the original three acres of Ellis Island, but the two states disagreed about who owned the other twenty-four. It was a matter of some practical, as well as symbolic, importance, because the island had become home to a small number of permanent inhabitants, was the site of some taxable commercial activity, and was a place where a not-inconsequential number of people were born, got married, and died. Matters came to a head in the late 1980s. A government maintenance worker on Ellis Island who got part of his leg cut off by a stump-grinding machine sued the machine's manufacturer. For various arcane technical reasons, the worker's case turned on whether the law of New York or the law of New Jersey applied to his suit. A federal appellate court ruled that New York law applied. This was great for the worker, who could then recover for his injuries, but it did not bode well for New Jersey, which had assumed that its law applied to events happening on the island. At this point, New Jersey figured it was time to do something.

But what could it do? In some other time and place, perhaps New Jersey could have threatened New York with war, mobilized its tanks, and amassed troops along the border (if it could have figured out where that border was). Since that was not an option, maybe New Jersey could have challenged New York to a game of rock-paper-scissors. Again, not an option. Could New Jersey sue New York? But where? In what court? New Jersey would want the case heard in New Jersey; New York would say the case should be in New York. It's unlikely that courts in either state would be impartial. So what then? Sue in Connecticut? Burkina Faso? Luckily, the framers of the Constitution had foreseen precisely this problem, and so they provided right there in the founding document that states can sue each other directly in the Supreme Court of the United States. New Jersey's lawyers put on their best gray suits, shined up their briefcases, and headed down to 1 First Street.

Like the two articles before it, Article III of the Constitution begins with a so-called vesting clause: "The judicial Power of the United States, shall be vested in one supreme Court, and in such inferior Courts as the Congress may from time to time ordain and establish." You'll note that Article III gets odd very quickly. Not only does the phrase "from time to time" seem strange in something so grand as the world's greatest legal document ever (it seems more appropriate when describing your drinking or crack-smoking habits to a doctor), but isn't it also odd that the Constitution requires only that there be *one* federal court in the entire country? Whether to create other federal courts was left up to Congress. As it happened, Congress used its power under Article III to create lower federal courts in 1789, and they've existed ever since. The federal judicial system now consists primarily of ninety-four trial courts known as district courts, thirteen geographically based appellate courts that sit in panels of three and are known as circuit courts (so-named because they used to be staffed by Supreme Court justices, who would ride "circuit" around the geographical area, deciding cases), and of course the one Supreme Court with its marble steps and golden doors and swing justice Anthony Kennedy, who, as I've already pointed out, decides what the law is for every single person in the country all by his lonesome.

Article III is short—much shorter than Articles I or II—but it has some important stuff in it. For one thing, it limits the jurisdiction of the federal courts to deciding "cases" and "controversies," which is the origin of the depressing "standing" doctrine that I discussed in chapter 1. For another, it provides that all federal judges "shall hold their offices during good Behaviour, and shall, at stated Times, receive for their Services, a Compensation, which shall not be diminished during their Continuance in Office." In other words, federal judges, once appointed and confirmed, cannot be fired (they can be impeached, but that's something different—it's hard to do and very rare) or have their salary reduced. The idea behind life tenure and salary protection is that judges should be isolated from politics, so they can make decisions without worrying about whether the president or somebody else might fire them or cut their salary if their decisions turn out to be politically unpalatable. Being a federal judge, as you can see, is a sweet gig.

The tenure and salary-protection requirements of Article III raise an important issue—namely, if all people who exercise federal judicial power are supposed to have life tenure and salary protection, how come there are thousands of people out there exercising federal judicial power who do not have life tenure and salary protection? I'm sorry, *what?* Did the author just say that the government is unconstitutional? Well, maybe. Administrative agencies are filled with commissions and panels and even flat-out judges (called administrative law judges, or ALJs) who resolve disputes between individuals and the government, oftentimes following hearings that look a lot like trials, but who can be fired or given a pay cut. Add to these guys the judges of the so-called Tax Court and federal magistrate judges, and you've got a whole lot of people in the federal government exercising real judicial power who do not enjoy life tenure or salary protection. This problem has not eluded Supreme Court attention, but in a bunch of cases that are about as clear as a bowl of New England clam chowder, the Court has said that these arrangements are for the most part okay, either because "Article III judges" (those who enjoy life tenure and salary protection) review their decisions or because resolving disputes between the government and individuals (as opposed to disputes just among individuals) isn't the kind of judicial power the Constitution is talking about when it says "judicial power" or maybe just because there are so many of these non–Article III judges out there that if the Supreme Court held they were unconstitutional, the government would fall apart.

The Constitution also has a lot to say about what kinds of cases the federal courts, particularly the Supreme Court, can hear. According to Article III, the federal courts have jurisdiction to hear cases arising under federal law; cases between citizens of different states or between two states themselves; cases where the United States sues a state or where a state sues an individual of a different state; and cases involving foreign ambassadors, consuls, or ministers, among others. Notice that most kinds of cases—those routine matters where one person sues another person in the same state for selling a shipment of rotten cantaloupes or cutting off the wrong leg during an operation or not paying rent or whatever—cannot generally be heard by the federal courts; these cases lie solely within the jurisdiction of the state courts, which are created and governed by state law.

Next, Article III provides that the Supreme Court has two kinds of jurisdiction: original and appellate. In original-jurisdiction cases, the plaintiff sues the defendant directly in the Supreme Court without going to any other court first. With appellate jurisdiction, the plaintiff first sues in the trial court; the loser at that level may appeal to the circuit court, and the loser in the circuit court can ask the Supreme Court to take the case, which may or may not agree to hear it. Most of the Court's cases are brought under its appellate jurisdiction. Only a few types of cases can be brought under the Court's original jurisdiction, and those are specified by Article III's "original-jurisdiction clause": *In all Cases affecting Ambassadors, other public Ministers and Consuls, and those in which a State shall be Party, the supreme Court shall have original Jurisdiction.*

Very early on, Congress tried to expand the original jurisdiction of the Supreme Court. This did not work. Probably the most important case ever decided by the Court was *Marbury v. Madison,* which is significant mostly because that's where the Court announced that it could exercise "judicial review," meaning that courts can review laws passed by Congress to make sure they are constitutional. But the actual holding of the case is that Congress may not expand the original jurisdiction of the Supreme Court.

THE ODD CLAUSES *63*

After losing the election of 1800 to Thomas Jefferson, John Adams, determined to entrench his policies before Jefferson could take over, nominated a hefty group of justices of the peace in the District of Columbia. After the Senate confirmed the new judges, Adams's secretary of state (who happened to be John Marshall, also the chief justice of the Supreme Court) sent his brother to deliver signed commissions to the judges. One of these judges was William Marbury, but, sadly (from Marbury's perspective), he did not receive his commission before Jefferson took over as president. When Jefferson told his secretary of state, James Madison, to withhold the commissions, Marbury was basically screwed. Marbury then sued Madison directly in the Supreme Court, claiming that Congress had passed a statute giving the Court the power to order Madison to deliver the commission to Marbury. The Supreme Court dismissed the suit. In an opinion written by John Marshall, the Court held that no matter what Congress says, the only cases that can be brought under the Supreme Court's original jurisdiction are those that are specifically listed in Article III. Marbury lost, spent a happy life as a rich banker instead of a judge, and lived in a mansion that now houses the Ukrainian Embassy to the United States.

Although Congress cannot directly change the original jurisdiction of the Supreme Court, it *can* give lower federal courts concurrent jurisdiction over the same cases that the Supreme Court can hear under its original jurisdiction. And indeed, Congress has done precisely that for almost all of the types of cases listed by Article III as falling under the Supreme Court's original jurisdiction. Specifically, Congress has said that the federal trial courts can hear cases involving ambassadors, ministers, or consuls; cases between the United States and a state; and cases brought by a state against citizens of a different state. For these kinds of cases, then, the parties will go to the trial court first instead of the Supreme

Court. This is perfectly fine with the Supreme Court, it's worth noting, because the Court is not set up to hold trials in any way. The justices are used to deciding cases on appeal, which means reading a lot of papers and thinking about weighty issues and having a short oral argument where they can ask the lawyers questions or badger them or show off how funny they think they are or whatever, but they are not equipped to hear witnesses or entertain objections ("Objection, Justices, the witness is not an oral surgeon!") or listen to days and days of arguments about all sorts of minor issues, which is what judges have to do when they preside over a trial. Indeed, the Court would most likely be quite happy to never have to exercise its original jurisdiction at all. Unfortunately for the Court, however, there is one type of case that Congress has not allowed lower federal courts to hear—cases brought by one state against another state. For these cases, no other court would have the authority or the objectivity necessary to provide a fair trial. When a state sues another state, then, it has to come directly to the Supreme Court.

I have always found these cases where one state sues another state to be fascinating. I think it has something to do with how the case names sound like college football games: *Missouri vs. Illinois, Arkansas vs. Oklahoma, Kansas vs. Colorado.* I've wanted to write something about them for a long time. A while back, I asked one of my favorite colleagues, a professor named Larry Yackle (that's "YAKE-il," as in "Shake-il" or "Bake-il," not "Tackle"), if he wanted to cowrite a book with me called *State versus State: The Ten Greatest State against State Cases in Supreme Court History,* which, granted, would have made for one hell of an awful book, but I still think it's a testimony to how serious legal academics tend to be that even Yackle—who brings his dog into work on the front of his Vespa—just looked at me like I was an idiot when I made the suggestion and walked away.

The Supreme Court does not hear many state-versus-state cases—maybe one or two per year at the most. It doesn't even hear all the cases brought by states against other states. Somewhat controversially, it has said that it will only hear such cases when "the threatened invasion of rights . . . is of serious magnitude." So, for example, in 1981, the Court refused to hear a case brought by California against West Virginia alleging that the latter had breached a contract involving a football game between the West Virginia Mountaineers and the San Jose State Spartans; the Court, apparently, thought that the controversy lacked sufficient seriousness. It's not clear that the Court should have the discretion to dismiss such cases. Sure, if one of the parties is not actually a state, it makes sense for the Court to dismiss the case, as it did when Illinois tried to sue Milwaukee (not a state) or when Mississippi was sued by the Principality of Monaco (again, not a state). But when one real state sues another real state, Justice Stevens, who dissented in the California versus West Virginia decision, might have had it right when he said that the Court has no discretion to refuse to hear such a dispute.

So, why do states sue each other? The cases fall into several categories. Like the Ellis Island case, many of these disputes involve borders. One state thinks its property extends to the thirty-third parallel or whatever, and its neighboring state disagrees. States want more land so they can collect more tax money and claim more residents, thereby maybe getting some more representation in Congress, and so the state that thinks it should have more property sues the other state. A few examples: Rhode Island sued Massachusetts in the 1830s over land next to Narragansett Bay; Indiana sued Kentucky over something called the Green River Island in the late nineteenth century; Missouri sued both Nebraska and Kansas over various pieces of land in the early twentieth century, and then Kansas sued Missouri over a different piece of land in the middle of the twentieth century. In 1913 New Mexico sued Texas over their boundary. Both states agreed that the border was defined by where the Rio Grande was in 1850, but they disagreed about exactly where this was. New Mexico put forth the testimony of witnesses who claimed to know where the river had traveled back then, but the testimony was rejected as unreliable, since the witnesses were "old men, some very old," who hadn't been on the river for sixty years, and even then had generally traveled in the dark because "in those years the country was wild and infested with hostile Indians." In the early 1970s, in what *Time* magazine referred to as a "boiling dispute," Maine patrol officers arrested a New Hampshire lobsterman for fishing in Maine waters. Believing that Maine had overstepped its boundaries, New Hampshire's governor announced that "Maine has declared war on us!" and brought suit in the Court, which ended up ruling (sort of) for Maine.

A second big group of cases involve water rights of various types. Many of the cases are about which state gets to use some body of water. Wyoming once sued Colorado over the Laramie River; Wisconsin once sued Illinois over parts of Lake Michigan; Connecticut sued Massachusetts over the Connecticut River; New Jersey sued New York over the Delaware River; and so on. A dispute between Nebraska and Wyoming over certain rights to the North Platte River went in and out of the Court for over sixty years. Other cases involve pollution. Did New Jersey have the right to throw sewage into New York harbor and cause "offensive odors"? Did New York have the right to create a giant sludge bed in Lake Champlain, or did this violate Vermont's sovereignty?

One of the most fascinating state-versus-state cases of all time took place at the very beginning of the twentieth century, when the Sanitary District of Chicago reversed the flow of the Chicago River in order to send its contaminated sewage water down the Mississippi River rather than into Lake Michigan. This was great for the residents of Chicago, but not so terrific for the citizens of St. Louis, where it was alleged that the arrival of "1500 tons of poisonous filth per day" had caused a typhus epidemic. Missouri sued Illinois, on the theory that the Sanitary District was an agent of the state. The first question was whether the Court would even entertain a suit like this; on that question, the Court said absolutely. In Justice Holmes's words: "The nuisance set forth in the bill was one which would be of international importance—a visible change of a great river from a pure stream into a polluted and poisoned ditch. The only question presented was whether, as between the states of the Union, this court was competent to deal with a situation which, if it arose between independent sovereignties, might lead to war. . . . [T]he jurisdiction and authority of this court to deal with such a case as that is not open to doubt." At the same time, though, the Court was worried about opening its doors to every claim that one state had polluted the waters of another state; it decided, therefore, that before it would intervene, "the case should be of serious magnitude, clearly and fully proved." Examining the evidence before it in great detail—not only the typhoid statistics from St. Louis over the relevant period, but also experiments regarding the likelihood that typhus bacteria could survive the long journey from the Windy to the Gateway City—the Court concluded that the evidence was insufficient for it to act, and it dismissed Missouri's complaint. St. Louis, I'm afraid, hasn't been the same since.

Tax disputes make up a third set of cases. My favorite cases within this category are those where the plaintiff state and the defendant state are far away from each other. If the boundary and water-rights cases resemble college football matchups between teams from the same conference, then cases involving distant states are like the games where a team from the

ACC plays a school from the Big Ten. One of these cases involved a claim by California against Texas for the right to tax the estate of Howard Hughes, but that case actually turns out to be quite boring. A far more interesting case is *Texas v. Florida et al.*, where Texas sued Florida, Massachusetts, and New York because it thought that Edward H.R. Green, the rich son of a prominent Massachusetts whaling family who died in New York in the mid-1930s, had been "domiciled" in Texas at his death, thus giving Texas rather than these other states the right to tax his estate. The Court had to decide which of these four states best represented Green's home, in the sense of where he spent most of his time and where he intended to stay in the future. Analyzing the facts of Green's life in excruciating detail, the justices found that Green's real domicile at his death was Massachusetts, where he had built a $7 million estate, complete with "swimming pools, tennis courts, radio broadcasting stations, an airport, airship hangar and dock." In the Court's view, this investment, along with the fact that Green spent more time in Massachusetts than in any other state during his later years, trumped his connections with the other states, even though he did spend the winters in Florida (often on a houseboat) and continued to his dying day to say that he was a resident of Texas, where he had lived for twenty years earlier in his life and thereafter had even rented a room (occupied only by "a box containing a pair of trousers and a vest"). Inexplicably, the Court did not inquire into why anyone would ever want to wear a vest in Texas.

Okay, so by now you get the point that I like these cases because they remind me of college football games. At one point while working on this book, I thought it would be fun to figure out which states have brought the most original-jurisdiction cases, which have had the most cases brought against them, and which states have done the best and worst in terms of their won-loss records. I envisioned a standings chart like you see for the NFL in the newspaper. To put my plan into effect, I went to my computer legal database and pulled up all the state-versus-state cases from our two-hundred-plus-year history. There are a lot of them. I started making notes. I worked on the project for maybe an hour and a half. I got through about three of the cases (some of these old cases are hard to read). Then I decided, *Who the hell am I kidding, I have a family, my editor is a stickler about her deadlines, I'm not doing this.* And then I went home.

I mentioned before that the justices of the Supreme Court would probably prefer not to hear any original-jurisdiction cases at all, because the Court is set up to consider cases on appeal, which means that by the time it gets the case, the lower courts have already sifted through the testimony and evidence and figured out what actually happened. The Supreme Court doesn't generally busy itself with this painstaking task; instead it focuses primarily on deciding purely legal issues (e.g., Does the Clean Air Act allow agencies to weigh costs and benefits when setting pollution standards? Does the equal-protection clause require states to allow gay marriage? Does the thirty-day clock governing removal of actions from state to federal court contained in 28 U.S.C. § 1446(b) start running when the defendant is officially served with a complaint, or might it begin earlier, such as when the defendant receives a faxed copy of that document?). In original-jurisdiction cases, however, there is no lower court to sift through the facts, so the Supreme Court has to sort through them itself. Theoretically, the justices could do this by holding their own trials, but while the Court has done this three times in its history, its practice these days is almost invariably to delegate its fact-finding duties to an experienced individual known as a "special master."

Special masters do everything that a trial judge typically would do in a case, and then some. Almost no rules constrain the ability of the special master from discovering every fact that might be potentially relevant to deciding the case. Special masters preside over trials, call witnesses themselves (trial judges rarely do this), take evidence, collect documents, consider procedural motions, rule on objections, and do countless other things to investigate everything having to do with the dispute. After the trial is over and the evidence is all collected, the special master prepares something called a "finding of facts" laying out exactly what he (and I do mean "he"—the Court didn't appoint a female special master until January 2008) thinks happened and then ultimately renders a tentative decision in the case that goes up to the Court for its review. Just to get a sense for how much work is involved in one of these cases, consider the Ellis Island controversy, where the special master collected two thousand documents, compiled four thousand pages of testimony, held a trial in one of the side rooms of the Supreme Court that lasted twenty-three days and involved the testimony of twenty-one witnesses, and then prepared a nearly two-hundred-page report summarizing his findings and putting forth his recommendations for the Court.

So, who are these special masters anyway? And, moreover, why hasn't the author—who clearly has a keen interest in these cool cases—been appointed one yet? Sometimes the Court appoints prominent academics like the dean of a major law school (not, in other words, a barely tenured professor who spends his time writing books about weird clauses of the Constitution). The special master in the Ellis Island case, for instance, was Paul Verkuil, who has been the dean at both Tulane Law School and Cardozo Law School in New York City. Other times the justices choose a prominent private lawyer to serve as special master; this can be a problem, however, because these lawyers are incredibly expensive. The states involved in the suit generally split the cost of the special master, which can run up into the seven figures if the justices choose a partner at a big-city law firm. Finally, the justices have often chosen retired or senior judges to serve as special masters. Indeed, on three occasions, a former Supreme Court justice has served in the position, the most recent time being when former justice Tom Clark was appointed to serve as the special master in the aforementioned "boiling dispute" between Maine and New Hampshire over lobster-fishing rights.

Critics, including even some sitting justices, have occasionally called into question the use of special masters by the Supreme Court in original-jurisdiction cases. The money thing is one prominent critique; another is that special masters have too much power and freedom to do whatever they want. Those who voice the latter objection argue that the Supreme Court, or perhaps Congress, should come up with specific rules and regulations to better constrain them. There's even an argument that the special master position—because it authorizes people who do not enjoy life tenure and salary protection to exercise a sort of "judicial power"—violates Article III of the Constitution.

In my view, these objections are overstated. The only one with any real weight is the argument that using a big-firm private lawyer costs the litigating states an excessive amount, but this can be solved either by hiring public officials to serve as special masters or by refusing to pay law-firm rates to private lawyers who serve in the position. No, my main problem with using special masters is that it's just no fun. Sure, I get it. The Court is used to reviewing decisions of other courts, so it appoints a special master to essentially act as a lower court. But wouldn't it be way more exciting if the justices went back to holding trials themselves? Maybe they could do them in the summer, when the justices aren't doing anything anyway except skipping away on boondoggles to places like Madrid and Reykjavik. I'd love to see the justices arguing with each other about whether to let in a piece of evidence or to grant an objection. Here's how I imagine it playing out:

In a crowded courtroom, while the nine justices look on, each with his or her own gavel, a lawyer examines a witness.

LAWYER: So, why did the rich dead man whose property both states want spend his winters in Florida?

WITNESS: Well, the cold weather exacerbated his temporomandibular joint discomfort.

OPPOSING LAWYER: Objection, the witness is not an oral surgeon!

The bench erupts. Everyone yells at once, banging gavels.

JUSTICES ALITO, KENNEDY, ROBERTS, AND SCALIA: Objection granted.

JUSTICES BREYER, GINSBURG, SOTOMAYOR, AND KAGAN: Objection overruled.

JUSTICE SCALIA *[biting his gavel in half]*: Overruled? Are you kidding? Liberal fools.

JUSTICE BREYER: As I see it, this objection raises a fascinating theoretical issue. Imagine, if you will, that . . .

Justice Breyer talks nonstop about various things nobody understands for about ten minutes.

JUSTICE KENNEDY: This is hard, no doubt about it. Maybe the objection should be overruled after all. No, I guess it should be granted. No, overruled. No, granted. Definitely granted. Unless . . .

JUSTICE SOTOMAYOR: As a Latina woman, I think I see this issue differently from the rest of you. I say overruled!

JUSTICE ROBERTS: It looks like we're deadlocked. Justice Thomas, you are the deciding vote. What do you think?

Silence.

JUSTICE ROBERTS: Clarence? Hello.

Nothing.

Okay, enough of this.

Remember all those millions of immigrants who entered the United States through Ellis Island? Well, it turns out they all landed in New Jersey. There is an ancient and universally followed legal rule called the rule of "avulsion," which, when applied to a situation like this, says that when additional territory is added to an island by fill material, the added area belongs not to the party that owns the island but to the party that controls the water where the fill material was added. In other words, since the US government enlarged the island by adding dirt and rocks to the water around the original three-acre Ellis Island, and since the water around that original island was controlled by New Jersey under the 1834 compact, the twenty-four acres of land added to the island belonged to New Jersey and not New York.

Figuring that the avulsion rule would work to New Jersey's favor, New York had advanced a second argument in the case, which was that even if New Jersey originally owned the added twenty-four acres, New York nonetheless gained sovereignty over that land because it had *acted as though* it had sovereignty over it for a long period of time without any objection from New Jersey. Unfortunately for New York, however, the special master concluded—and the Court agreed—that New York's evidence on this score was paltry at best. The Court was not impressed, for example, that New York had recorded five birth certificates of babies born on Ellis Island during the sixty-four years between when the federal government started adding land to the island and the time that New Jersey clearly started to assert that it had sovereignty over the filled portions. New York also tried to argue that over those sixty-four years, most people *thought* Ellis Island was in New York. This actually might have been relevant, said the Court, but it nonetheless found that New York had failed to put forth a strong enough showing. For example, the Court was not wowed by the testimony of "one William Hewitt, who lived in the officers' quarters on the Island with his family from July to September 1940 when he was one year old [and] testified that although he had 'no personal recollection of living on the Island, he has always thought that at that time he was living in New York.'" And although a dissenting Justice Stevens thought the "New York" labeled landing cards and the like were sufficient to show that most people thought the island was in New York, the majority was unconvinced, since the "New York" on those documents referred to the "New York Immigration District," which at the time included northern New Jersey.

The framers sure knew what they were doing when they created the Constitution. One of the big risks of bringing together a bunch of strong, independent states in one unified country was that inevitably there would be times when the states would not get along. The framers knew that states would struggle and compete and disagree with each other over all sorts of things, and they tried to take steps to limit the chance that these disagreements would erupt into outright conflict and violence. A number of constitutional provisions serve this purpose. Article I, Section 8, gives the federal government the power to regulate interstate commerce; a corollary of this power, as the Supreme Court has long recognized, is that individual states themselves cannot regulate interstate commerce. The "dormant commerce clause," as it's known, prevents states from using their regulatory power to discriminate against goods from other states. A state, for example, that prohibited the sale of out-of-state oranges within its borders to protect its in-state citrus industry would soon find itself on the losing end of a constitutional controversy. Likewise, the so-called full faith and credit clause of Article IV provides that judicial judgments made in one state must be given full effect in other states. Someone who is found negligent by a jury in Arkansas, for instance, cannot move to Missouri and expect to find refuge.

The original-jurisdiction clause, then, is one of a number of crucial constitutional provisions meant to secure peace among the several states. Of course, the United States was almost torn apart irrevocably in the 1860s by the Civil War, and so we can't say that the original-jurisdiction clause has fully prevented interstate conflict. It is, however, hard to imagine that anything could have prevented the Civil War, and apart from that war, and putting aside the governor of New Hampshire's melodramatic proclamation about Maine's assault on his state's lobstermen, the United States has remained remarkably free from real interstate conflict. Part of the reason surely lies in the original-jurisdiction clause, which lets aggrieved states take their cases directly to the highest court in the land, an objective court with no direct connection to any particular state. Most people in the United States probably don't even know about the original-jurisdiction clause, but that doesn't mean it's not important. On the contrary, the clause's inconspicuousness is evidence of how well it works. The original-jurisdiction clause is one of those parts of the Constitution that goes about its business quietly—oddly and quietly—performing a critical function for our nation.

CHAPTER 5

The Natural-Born Citizen Clause

Elected Office for (Almost) Anyone!

No person except a natural born Citizen, or a Citizen of the United States, at the time of the Adoption of this Constitution, shall be eligible to the Office of President.

Article II, Section 1

In the mid-1990s, a couple of hot-shot legal academics were walking back to their hotel after taking part in a constitutional law conference at Tulane University when they started talking about what they thought was the "stupidest" part of the Constitution. Since these guys are law professors, it should be no surprise that they quickly decided to turn their "joking conversation" into an eighty-five-page academic symposium. They called up a bunch of their top-notch law professor friends around the country and asked them what they thought was the stupidest part of the Constitution. By "stupidest," the study's designers meant (we learn in the symposium's first footnote) "a provision that strikes one as wrongheaded under *today's* circumstances, and harmful to the polity as well." In other words, to be stupid, a provision had to cause problems in 1995, regardless of what it might have done back in 1787 or 1791 or whenever it was first ratified. As one symposium participant put it, the chosen phrase or clause or section "should be something you think has significance for current governance; you get no points by condemning the fugitive slave clause." Contributors were encouraged not to talk to other participants about their choices, so that each could select his or her favorite "constitutional stupidity" without being subject to undue influence from external forces.

Although some of the participants responded with typical academic tomfoolery like refusing to answer the question directly or attacking the question itself (note, e.g., the response of one professor, who called the enterprise "the most vapid essay contest to come along since MTV listeners were asked to suggest names for a new litter of puppies owned by a heavy metal performer"), for the most part the study turned out to be enlightening. Which parts of the Constitution were the biggest losers? One was the provision in Article III that gives federal judges life tenure. As one critic observed: "Life tenure . . . creates the real possibility of imitating a society like China, where power is wielded by the oldest among it." The electoral college earned a couple of votes for making it possible for someone like George W. Bush to become president despite getting five hundred thousand fewer popular votes than his opponent. And lots of scorn was heaped atop the provision in Article I that gives each state two votes in the Senate, regardless of whether the state has the eighth-largest economy in the world (like California) or can fit in the palm of a toddler's hand (like Rhode Island).

Getting at least as many votes as any other clause was the clause in Article II that prohibits anyone who is not a "natural born citizen" from becoming the president. In this chapter, I will talk about where this clause came from, what it means, and why one participant in the stupidity symposium called it "a vestigial excrescence on the face of our Constitution."

⟋⟍

As I mentioned in chapter 3, the Constitution sets out detailed rules about how officers of the United States are to be appointed to their positions. The Constitution, however, generally does not create these offices itself; most offices are created by statute. In a few important cases, though, the Constitution does actually create offices. For these offices—the president, the vice president, senators, and members of the House of Representatives—the Constitution not only establishes the position and provides the method for filling it (by election), but it also sets forth specific qualifications that anyone occupying the position has to have.

What is most notable about these prerequisites is just how few of them there actually are. They are also pretty minor. Most are simple age and residency requirements: you need to be at least thirty-five years old and have lived in the country for fourteen years to be president or vice president, thirty years old with nine years in the country to be a senator, and only twenty-five with seven years of residency to be in the House. The Constitution does not require that officers have to come from a certain lineage or have achieved a certain level of education or belong to any particular religious faith. Indeed, the "religious test clause" of Article VI flatly prohibits the government from requiring any religious test for any "Office or public Trust under the United States."

It was no accident that the framers insisted on only the most minimal qualifications for high public office. Keeping these prerequisites to a minimum furthered two values that the framers believed were vitally important. The first was equality—the notion that anyone (well, any white man, that is) could aspire to elected office, even someone with no land, the measliest education, and the weirdest religious views. As James Madison said in *The Federalist Papers,* No. 52: "The door of this part of the federal government is open to merit of every description, whether native or adoptive, whether young or old, and without regard to poverty or wealth, or to any particular profession of religious faith." The second value was representativeness—the idea that when people go to the polls, they should be able to elect whomever they want to represent them. These two values were so strongly championed by the nation's founders that when the Supreme Court in 1995 considered the constitutionality of state-imposed term limits for US representatives, the Court pointed to them when finding that the short list of qualifications contained in the Constitution were intended to be exclusive. Since that list contains no limits on the amount of time a Representative can serve, the Court struck down an Arkansas law banning ballot access to anyone who had previously served three terms in the House.

What about the qualifications that *are* constitutionally required? The age requirements seem very straightforward. Justice Felix Frankfurter once called the thirty-five-year minimum age requirement for president one of the most "explicit and specific" provisions in the whole document, astutely observing that it "draws on arithmetic." The supposed clarity of these provisions, however, has made them a favorite topic among people who like to argue about how the Constitution ought to be interpreted. One of the big issues in constitutional interpretation is whether the words of the text have a clear and fixed meaning that judges should mechanically apply or whether at least some parts of the document are ultimately indeterminate and therefore require judicial creativity (i.e., judgment) to apply. Most of this indeterminacy debate centers around the at least relatively loosey-goosey language of the Constitution's lions, tigers, and bears—the First Amendment, for example, which prohibits laws "respecting an establishment of religion," or the Eighth Amendment, which bars the infliction of "cruel and unusual punishments."

In these debates over interpretation, the age provisions are often held up as examples that, at least some of the time, the framers knew how to create very clear rules. How much clearer can it get, it's suggested, than saying that the president has to be at least thirty-five years old? For some of your more ardent supporters of constitutional indeterminacy, though, the age provisions have simply provided a spirited challenge. After all, if it is possible to show that even the "you have to be thirty-five to be president" clause is not entirely clear, then it is a good bet that phrases like "establishment of religion" or "cruel and unusual punishments" are clam chowdery as well. If that's true, then judges might be more comfortable applying these phrases to stop the government, for instance, from leading Christian prayers or electrocuting prisoners or engaging in other nauseating practices that the Constitution does not expressly prohibit.

Given the prominence of these debates, it shouldn't be surprising to learn that legal scholars have come up with all kinds of theories about why "thirty-five" might not really mean "thirty-five." One typical argument goes something like this. When the framers said "thirty-five," what they meant was that to be president a candidate must possess a "certain level of maturity" or a "minimum level of maturity and experience." The arbitrary choice of "thirty-five" was simply intended as a shorthand for this more general principle. Thus, perhaps a particularly mature and experienced thirty-four-year-old could ascend to the presidency. A slightly different version of the argument extends the point, suggesting that we need to translate the principle from its eighteenth-century context to contemporary times, in which children arguably mature at a very different rate from earlier days. This leads to its own problems. Do children mature more quickly than they used to, or less? Does better access to education and information mean that people are ready to take on the presidency earlier than before (say, when they're thirty) or does the relatively late assumption these days of adult obligations like employment, marriage, and parenthood argue in favor of raising the minimum age to something more like forty (or eighty)?

Okay, fine, you might say—perhaps it's not entirely ridiculous to suggest that an experienced thirty-four-year-old should be able to become president. But certainly the Constitution prohibits someone who is, say, eighteen, from becoming president, right? *Aha,* say the constitutional-indeterminacy people, this is only because the facts of the world as we know them right now make it absurd to contemplate an eighteen-year-old president. What if these facts changed dramatically, though? Would you still be so confident in refusing to extend the language of the Constitution to allow an eighteen-year-old into office if, as one legal scholar posits, "an unstoppable virus causes the death of all persons over twenty-years old"? Or what if, as one of the nation's most prominent legal academics has suggested, a teenage guru appears whose "supporters sincerely claim that their religion includes among its tenets a belief in reincarnation"? I mean, the guru says he's forty-two-thousand years old, and you're going to claim he can't be president? Does it matter that the First Amendment prohibits discrimination on the basis of religion? Does it matter that the equal-protection clause of the Fourteenth Amendment arguably prohibits discrimination on the basis of age? Does it matter that both of these amendments postdate the main body of the Constitution, where the "thirty-five" clause is found?

Constitutional interpretation is a can of worms.

Among the constitutional provisions that create officer qualifications, the one proverbial turd in the punchbowl is the natural-born citizen clause of Article II: *No person except a natural born Citizen, or a Citizen of the United States at the time of the Adoption of this Constitution, shall be eligible to the Office of President.* The clause, described by critics as "highly objectionable," "inane," "blatantly discriminatory," "morally dubious," and a "lowdown dirty shame," is the only place in the Constitution—indeed, perhaps, in all of American law—where a distinction is drawn between naturalized citizens and those born in the United States.

As is often the case, the framers didn't say much about why they put the natural-born citizen clause into the Constitution. The source of the restriction, though, is generally traced back to a letter that John Jay, who would become the nation's first chief justice, sent to George Washington in 1787. Jay wrote: "Permit me to hint whether it would be wise and seasonable to provide a strong check to the admission of foreigners into the administration of our national government and to declare expressly that the commander in chief of the American army shall not be given to, nor devolve on, any but a natural born citizen." It's been said that Jay was responding to rumors that a foreign prince, such as Baron Von Steuben, the Prussian aristocrat who helped train the Revolutionary army, would be asked to serve as president. As the great nineteenth-century scholar and Supreme Court justice Joseph Story put it, the clause was intended to cut off "all chances for ambitious foreigners, who might otherwise be intriguing for the office."

The clause is flawed for a whole of bunch of different reasons. For one, it's hypocritical. Notice how the clause makes an exception for non-natural-born citizens at the time the Constitution was adopted; the United States didn't have a natural-born citizen president until Martin Van Buren took office in 1836. The clause also doesn't solve the problem it supposedly identifies. If someone who isn't a natural-born citizen can't be president, why can one of these untrustworthy scoundrels serve as secretary of state or chief justice of the Supreme Court or chairman of the Joint Chiefs of Staff or ambassador to the United Nations?

It is the principle of the thing, though, that's really bad. The fact that just about anybody growing up within the country's borders can aspire to someday hold the nation's highest position is one of the most admirable features of our constitutional system. But then there's this crazy provision that makes an exception for one group, and only one group, and says to members of that group: *No, not you, you cannot become president, you are not equal members of this community.* And why? Because people who become citizens are less likely to feel allegiance to the country than those who were citizens by birth? What a bizarre and unjustified assumption. What about those naturalized citizens who have lived in the United States practically their whole lives? What about those who have served in the government? In the military? As the guy who called the clause a vestigial excrescence on the face of our Constitution eloquently (if perhaps a bit melodramatically) put it:

> [A]t the very heart of the constitutional order, in the Office of the President, the Constitution abandons its brave experiment of forging a new society based upon principles of voluntary commitment; it instead gropes for security among ties of blood and contingencies of birth. In a world of ethnic cleansing, where affirmations of allegiance are drowned in attributes of status, this constitutional vision is a chilling reminder of a path not taken, of a fate we have struggled to avoid.

Then, of course, there's the practical problem that we've been excluding some truly excellent potential candidates from running for president. Take, for instance, Bob Hope, who was ridiculously popular during the middle part of the twentieth century among US troops and just about everyone else but who was born in England to English parents and so could never become president. More seriously, consider whether it makes any sense at all to exclude governors Jennifer Granholm or Arnold Schwarzenegger or former secretaries of state Madeleine Albright or Henry Kissinger from seeking the presidency. As another symposium participant wrote, "There are many reasons why Henry Kissinger should not have become President, but his having been born in Germany is certainly not one of them."

One person who has definitely never been barred from becoming president by the natural-born citizen clause is Barack Obama. Born in Hawaii in 1961, two years after it became a state, the nation's forty-fourth president is undoubtedly a natural-born citizen. Ask some large percentage of the American public, however—some polls have it higher than 20 percent—and you'll get a different opinion. The members of the so-called birther movement have all sorts of theories about why Obama is not a natural-born citizen. Some say he was born in Kenya. Or England. Or Indonesia. Or Russia. Some say he was smuggled into the United States as a baby. Some concede he was born in Hawaii but say it doesn't matter because his father was born in England, thus making Obama a dual citizen of the United States and England (which is irrelevant anyway, but never mind). Some say his real father was a communist poet, which has nothing to do with the natural-born-citizen controversy except that it purportedly explains why Obama has not released his Hawaiian birth certificate.

Except that Obama has released his birth certificate. Twice! First, he put a copy online during the 2008 presidential campaign. The birthers didn't believe it was real. Hawaii's health director and registrar of vital statistics confirmed both that the birth certificate was real and that it said what Obama said it said. The birthers didn't believe them. An independent organization called FactCheck.org, working out of the University of Pennsylvania, claimed to have seen, felt, and sniffed the actual birth certificate. The organization said it was real. The birthers weren't convinced. In April 2011, Obama finally released his actual birth certificate, bowing to pressure from a man with bad hair. Still, though, lots of people somehow continue to insist that Obama was born overseas.

Birthers have filed a series of lawsuits challenging Obama's presidency. So far, they've lost every one. Judges have tended to dismiss these lawsuits with great zeal. A federal district judge in Washington, DC, for instance, wrote of one challenge: "This case, if it were allowed to proceed, would deserve mention in one of those books that seek to prove that the law is foolish or that America has too many lawyers with not enough to do." Of a prominent birther attorney, a federal judge in California said: "Plaintiff's counsel has favored rhetoric seeking to arouse the emotions and prejudices of her followers rather than the language of a lawyer seeking to present arguments through cogent legal reasoning." This same lawyer was fined $20,000 by a judge in Georgia for abusing the judicial system. Apparently Judge Clay Land was not persuaded by the attorney's motions that "describe the President as a 'prevaricator,' allege that the President's father was 'disloyal and possibly treacherous' to the 'British Crown,' accuse the undersigned of treason, and suggest that the United States District Courts in this Circuit are 'subservient' to the 'illegitimate' 'de facto President.'" Citing "Yankee's baseball legend and philosopher Yogi Berra" for the proposition that "it was déjà vu all over again," and for using the term "frivolous" nine times in a seven-page order, Judge Land concluded, "Although the First Amendment may allow Plaintiff's counsel to make these wild accusations on her blog or in her press conferences, the federal courts are reserved for hearing genuine legal disputes and not as a platform for political rhetoric that is disconnected from any legitimate legal cause of action."

Personally, I have mixed feelings about the whole birther-movement thing. I mean, on the one hand, of course it's wasteful and disgusting and probably racist, but on the other, it does serve to make conservatives look silly, which has got to be worth something, right? Even some more or less mainstream conservatives realize how ludicrous these birthers are. As right-wing talk show host Michael Medved put it, the movement's leaders are "crazy, nutburger, demagogue, money-hungry, exploitative, irresponsible, filthy conservative imposters" who make people like him seem "sick, troubled, and not suitable for civilized company." *Nutburger!* Plus, some of these birthers' arguments are priceless. Here's one of my favorites, in which a "dualist" (someone who thinks Obama has dual citizenship and is thus ineligible for the presidency) explains to a "twit" from the *Huffington Post* the basics of the dualist position on Obama's legitimacy:

> Imagine a cat sneaks into the dog pound, and has a litter of kittens, Obama can issue orders not [to] offend the kittens by calling them kittens, [Arianna Huffington] and the rest of the MSM ["mainstream media"] can write op-eds decrying the injustice of forcing them to be kittens and not puppies, George Soros can buy scientists to say kittens are mammals just like puppies are mammals to influence a congressional votes [*sic*] to make them dogs, but nature and natures [*sic*] God is going to make them scratch the couch, cough up fur balls and meow all day long. They are 100% kittens, and more importantly they are 100% kittens by nature. Obama by nature is not 100% American and that is what this is all about.

You can't make this stuff up.

༄

Unlike Barack Obama, Republican senator John McCain was not born in the United States. He was born in the Panama Canal Zone in 1936 to parents who were both US citizens. Is McCain a natural-born citizen? If he had chosen a legitimate running mate and won the 2008 presidential election, could he have become president?

The question turns out to be tricky. The problem is that nobody knows exactly what it means to be a "natural-born citizen." Indeed, the most obvious reading of the phrase would suggest that only people who are born vaginally can ascend to the presidency. Nobody takes this view, of course, but apart from people who are actually born in one of the fifty states, it's not always clear who counts as a natural-born citizen (actually, even within the fifty states, things can get fuzzy—what about children of foreign ambassadors or enemy combatants?) For example, what about children of Native Americans born on reservations that are not subject to federal jurisdiction? What about children born in Guam or Puerto Rico? What about children whose nationality is unknown? What about children born on US military bases overseas? What about children—like John McCain—born outside the United States to parents who are both US citizens? As to all these questions, the answer is basically *who knows?* US immigration and citizenship law is notoriously confusing, and the Supreme Court has never provided any concrete guidance on these thorny issues.

The question of whether someone who is born outside the United States to citizen parents can become president has come up several times. For some reason, 1968 was a big year for natural-born-citizen controversies. Both Barry Goldwater, who was born in Arizona before it became a state, and George Romney (father of Mitt), who was born in Mexico to Mormon missionaries, ran for president in 1968. Some observers were worried about whether these guys could have become president, but since neither of them won, the question never got resolved. The issue was raised during the 2008 election as well, and the McCain team even asked a couple of super-prominent lawyers to provide their legal opinion on the matter. When Laurence Tribe (on the left) and Theodore Olson (on the right) submitted their joint memorandum arguing that McCain was a natural-born citizen, the Senate soon thereafter passed a resolution concurring with their conclusion.

The Tribe-Olson legal opinion advanced two main arguments for why McCain is a natural-born citizen. Both arguments are plausible, but they are by no means free from doubt. First, the memo argues that McCain is a natural-born citizen because the United States exercised sovereignty over the Panama Canal Zone, and therefore McCain was born within the United States for purposes of the natural-born citizen clause. The potential problem with this theory is a series of cases decided by the Supreme Court in the early twentieth century called the Insular Cases, in which the Court held that the Constitution does not apply in full to unincorporated territories (those not destined to become states) like the Panama Canal Zone or Guam or (at the time) the Philippines. The legal opinion doesn't address the Insular Cases, and as University of Arizona law professor and main McCain-isn't-a-natural-born-citizen-arguer Gabriel Chin suggests, if McCain is a natural-born citizen simply because the Panama Canal Zone was under the sovereignty of the United States in 1936, then millions of people born in the Philippines before 1946 and the Panama Canal Zone before 1979—as well as perhaps their children and grandchildren—would be US citizens, which is something nobody ever figured was the case.

Second, Tribe and Olson argue that the framers of the Constitution understood the phrase "natural born citizen" to include children of US citizens born abroad. Because the framers didn't explicitly address the question anywhere in the document itself or in its drafting history, though, the argument is based on inferences about what the state of the law was in England and the Colonies in 1787 regarding English citizenship, how much the framers knew about this law, and whether the framers (if they did know about it) intended to incorporate that law in the Constitution. These issues, it turns out, are hairy indeed. Legal scholars who have dived into the historical materials have surfaced with very different answers. It is true that the phrase "natural born citizen" echoes the phrase "natural born subjects" in English law at the time and that some laws of Parliament had extended the traditional notion of English citizenship (those born within the king's geographical realm) to children born outside the king's realm to parents who were subjects. On the other hand, as some have argued, it is far from clear that the American legal thinkers, founders, and colonial leaders at the time intended to import into the new nation English law created by Parliament in addition to the law handed down by English courts. And while it is true that a 1790 US statute provided that children born abroad to US citizens would themselves be considered natural-born citizens, this law could just as easily have represented a conscious *change* in how these children would be treated as it could have represented a *confirmation* of contemporary understandings (which is what the Tribe-Olson memo suggests).

This 1790 statute provides a third independent argument in favor of McCain's natural-born citizenship. The law, as it was amended in 1795 and read in 1936, granted US citizenship to any child "hereafter born out of the limits and jurisdiction of the United States" if at least one of the child's parents was a US citizen. Assuming that a statute like this can suffice to make someone a natural-born citizen under the Constitution (not altogether clear), whether it covers McCain turns on whether the Panama Canal Zone existed "out of the limits and jurisdiction of the United States" at the time of McCain's birth in 1936. Scholars disagree about this. In his article "Why Senator John McCain Cannot Be President: Eleven Months and a Hundred Yards Short of Citizenship," the aforementioned University of Arizona professor Gabriel Chin argues that the statute did not cover McCain because the Panama Canal Zone, while outside the *limits* of the United States, was not outside the *jurisdiction* of the United States. In response, a young scholar named Stephen Sachs has argued that the statute did cover McCain, suggesting among other things that the phrase "limits and jurisdiction" is a so-called legal "doublet," two words linked together that are not intended to have independent meanings, like "cease and desist" or "aid and abet" or "fair and balanced." In reply, Chin asks why, if people like McCain were covered by the 1795 law, Congress felt it necessary to pass a law in 1937 specifically providing that people born in the Panama Canal Zone to US citizen parents would thereafter be considered US citizens. It's a good question, particularly since it seems clear that members of Congress who advocated for the 1937 law believed that the Panama Canal Zone was, in the words of one member of the House of Representatives, "a no man's land"—not fully inside of the United States but not fully outside of it either.

So, is McCain a natural-born citizen, or not? If you ask me, I would say yes. That's because I believe that judges should interpret the Constitution pragmatically, looking to whether any particular interpretation makes sense in light of all the relevant circumstances, including not only the text of the document but also, in appropriate cases, to considerations of what is best for society. Because the language of the Constitution is ambiguous, and because it makes no sense to exclude people like McCain from the presidency, I would choose to interpret the natural-born citizen clause in a way that allows more people to become president rather than fewer people. Then again, however, McCain repeatedly stressed during the 2008 campaign that he prefers judges, like Justices Scalia and Thomas, who "strictly construe" the Constitution. So if McCain had won the election, and the Supreme Court had subsequently happened to use McCain's own preferred method of constitutional interpretation to bar him from the presidency, I wouldn't have shed any tears about it.

༚

Could someone who is clearly not a natural-born citizen ever carry out the duties of the president under our current Constitution? Surprisingly, perhaps, the answer may be yes, although getting there is a bit of a puzzle and would require Congress to pass one small statutory amendment, which it should proceed to do immediately. To figure this puzzle out, we have to look closely at the parts of the Constitution dealing with presidential succession.

Article II, Section 1, of the Constitution says that if the president dies, resigns, or becomes incapacitated, then the "Powers and Duties" of the presidency "shall devolve on the Vice President." This language was modified in 1967 by the Twenty-fifth Amendment, which says that, "In case of the removal of the President from Office or his death or resignation, the Vice President shall become President." Put these two provisions together, and you'll see that if the president dies or resigns, the vice president *becomes* the president, but if the president is merely incapacitated, the president remains the president, and his *duties devolve* on the vice president. In the language of other parts of the Constitution (the Twentieth, Twenty-second, and later sections of the Twenty-fifth amendments, for instance), this means that if the president is incapacitated, the vice president becomes the "acting" president rather than the actual president. Incidentally, one of the Constitution's super-odd provisions—Section 4 of the Twenty-fifth Amendment—provides that if the president and vice president disagree about whether the president is incapacitated, Congress gets to decide who will run the country (seriously, check it out).

What happens if both the president and the vice president die, resign, or become incapacitated? Anyone who is old enough to remember the 1981 assassination attempt on President Reagan will likely recall how Secretary of State Al Haig crazily wrongly announced that he was "in control" of the government pending the vice president's return to the White House. In fact, Haig was fourth in the line of succession, behind not only Vice President George H.W. Bush but also Speaker of the House Tip O'Neill and the president pro tempore of the Senate, Strom Thurmond. That's because under Article II, Section 1, of the Constitution, Congress "may by law provide for the Case of Removal, Death, Resignation or Inability, both of the President and Vice President, declaring what Officer shall then act as President." The statute passed by Congress under this section provides that if neither the president nor the vice president can discharge the president's duties, then the following officers, in this order, shall "act" as president:

> Speaker of the House, President pro tempore of the Senate, Secretary of State, Secretary of the Treasury, Secretary of Defense, Attorney General, Secretary of the Interior, Secretary of Agriculture, Secretary of Commerce, Secretary of Labor, Secretary of Health and Human Services, Secretary of Housing and Urban Development, Secretary of Transportation, Secretary of Energy, Secretary of Education, Secretary of Veterans Affairs, and Secretary of Homeland Security.

The natural-born citizen clause applies only to *becoming* the president, not to *acting* as president. The clause says that only a natural-born citizen is "eligible to the office" of president; presumably, then, someone who holds a different office (say, the secretary of state) while carrying out the duties of the president, does not have to be a natural-born citizen. Would it be okay for a vice president who is not a natural-born citizen to serve as an acting president in case the real president was incapacitated? Unfortunately, the Twelfth Amendment says that the vice president must also be a natural-born citizen (specifically, it says that "no person constitutionally ineligible to the office of President shall be eligible" to be the vice president), so this could never happen. But what about the other people on Congress's list? The Speaker of the House, for instance, or the secretary of veterans affairs?

Nothing in the Constitution prohibits any of these people from acting as president even if he or she is not a natural-born citizen. The problem, though, is that in the succession statute, Congress has provided that only officers who would be "eligible to the office of President under the Constitution" are authorized to act as president. In other words, if the president, vice president, Speaker of the House, president pro tempore of the Senate, and secretary of state were all dead, and the secretary of the treasury was not a natural-born citizen, then the secretary of defense would become the acting president rather than the secretary of the treasury. Here, it is *Congress,* rather than the *Constitution,* that has placed a disability on those citizens who were born outside the country.

In an ingenious article entitled "Unnatural Born Citizens and Acting Presidents" (to which I am much indebted for the above discussion), then law-firm lawyer and now (at this writing, anyway) the solicitor general of Texas, James C. Ho, argues that Congress should amend the succession statute to allow non-natural-born citizens to act as president in case both the president and vice president become unable to carry out the president's duties. As Ho, who himself is not a natural-born citizen, writes:

> Even such an incremental step . . . would at least allow the members of a previously excluded class of individuals some opportunity to prove that loyalty to the United States, the Constitution, and our founding principles of freedom and democracy is not the exclusive province of the native-born, by devolving presidential power to foreign-born citizens under relatively controlled conditions. . . .

Ho recognizes that this amendment would be a "very small step," but he also realizes the symbolic importance of the step—a step, as he says, that "would extend to millions of current and future mothers and fathers the distinctively American dream that their children might someday grow up to be (acting) President."

It's a brilliant suggestion. Congress should take Ho's advice, and pronto.

If the Fourteenth Amendment is a constitutional lion, and the incompatibility clause is a constitutional prairie dog, then the natural-born citizen clause is a constitutional Asian tiger mosquito, nutria rat, or zebra mussel. In other words, it is a pest. Pests need to be controlled. Ho's congressional solution is one small way to control it; judicial interpretation that limits the clause's scope is another way. But neither is sufficient. Even if judges limit the scope of what it means to be a "natural-born citizen" to those people clearly born outside US territory to parents who are not themselves US citizens, this still leaves many completely legitimate and highly qualified naturalized citizens forever excluded from seeking the presidency, and it still sends a symbolic message to these citizens that they are somehow second-class members of society.

For real constitutional pests like the natural-born citizen clause, nothing short of extinction through constitutional amendment will suffice. But getting rid of the clause will be about as easy as ridding the Great Lakes of zebra mussels. The framers purposely made it very difficult to amend our founding document; Article V provides that, among other things, three-fourths of the states have to ratify an amendment before it becomes part of the Constitution. As a result of this high bar for amendment, the Constitution has been amended only twenty-seven times in US history and only seventeen times since 1791. Still, though, it's probably worth a try. If it's good enough for the Sylvester Stallone–Sandra Bullock futuristic movie *Demolition Man,* in which it's revealed that Arnold Schwarzenegger became president as a result of the no-more-natural-born-citizen-requirement Sixty-first Amendment, then it should be good enough for real life too.

CHAPTER 6

The Twenty-first Amendment

Federalism

The transportation or importation into any State, Territory, or possession of the United States for delivery or use therein of intoxicating liquors, in violation of the laws thereof, is hereby prohibited.

Amendment XXI, Section 2

This may come as a surprise, but in the late 1960s, the problem of "bottomless" dancing in California bars and nightclubs had spiraled out of control. Or at least that was the opinion of the state's Department of Alcoholic Beverage Control, which became so worried about the menace that it held a series of public hearings to figure out the extent of the peril and what to do about it. The testimony at these hearings revealed, in the words of one federal court, a "sordid" story, "primarily relating to sexual contact between dancers and customers." Apparently, bottomless-dancing clubs were not nearly as wholesome as one might imagine. According to a different court: "Customers were found engaging in oral copulation with women entertainers; customers engaged in public masturbation; and customers placed rolled currency either directly into the vagina of a female entertainer, or on the bar in order that she might pick it up herself." The State of California, in other words, had turned into a Bangkok red-light district.

Of course, the state had already made it illegal for customers and dancers to engage in public sexual acts, but apparently those laws had not done the trick (so to speak). The agency in charge of licensing the sale of alcoholic beverages within the state therefore decided to do something about the bottomless dancing itself. It passed a series of regulations prohibiting a variety of lewd practices in any establishment selling liquor. Specifically, no club holding a liquor license could allow any person to perform acts of or simulating "sexual intercourse, masturbation, sodomy, bestiality, oral copulation, flagellation ... [or] the touching, caressing or fondling on the breast, buttocks, anus, or genitals." The state figured that banning these activities in bars would pretty much end them altogether; what guy, after all, is going to pay money to watch a woman simulate caressing her buttocks if he can't enjoy a beer at the same time?

The problem, however, was that California's regulations seemed clearly to violate the First Amendment. Fifteen or so years earlier, the Supreme Court had held that the government may not ban arguably profane speech or expression that does not rise to the level of "obscenity," with the term "obscenity" being very specifically defined as material that, when "taken as a whole," appeals to a "prurient" interest in sex and patently offends "community standards" relating to sex, while completely lacking any "social importance." Nothing in the regulations limited their application only to "obscene" instances of bestiality or flagellation. Accordingly, when a group of dancers and license holders sued to have the regulations invalidated, the three-judge lower federal court that heard the case held that the regulations were unconstitutional.

The Supreme Court, however, reversed. The Court agreed

that the "regulations on their face would proscribe some forms of visual presentation that would not be found obscene" under its prior cases. So why uphold the regulations? The answer appeared to rest in the language of Section 2 of the Twenty-first Amendment, which was ratified in 1933 to repeal the era of Prohibition that had been ushered in fourteen years earlier by the Eighteenth Amendment. According to the Court, Section 2 of the Twenty-first Amendment acted like a thumb on the scale of state power, giving states the authority to regulate alcohol in ways that would otherwise violate the Constitution. As the Court put it: "[T]he broad sweep of the Twenty-first Amendment has been recognized as conferring something more than the normal state authority over public health, welfare, and morals. . . . Given the added presumption in favor of the validity of the state regulation in this area that the Twenty-first Amendment requires, we cannot hold that the regulations on their face violate the Federal Constitution."

That seems like a strange result, doesn't it? How could the amendment that *ended* Prohibition be used by the Court to *uphold* a restriction on the sale of alcohol? Well, that depends on what the Twenty-first Amendment was all about. Was it about making alcohol legal, or was it about taking power over alcohol away from the federal government and returning it to the states, where it had always resided prior to 1919?

Perhaps the most difficult issue facing the framers of the Constitution was how to balance the powers of the new federal government with the powers of the states—to work out, in other words, the problem of federalism. Between the end of the Revolutionary War and the ratification of the Constitution, the newly independent states had been operating under the Articles of Confederation, a document that created a very limited federal government and left most powers to the states. This regime worked poorly, particularly because the states competed with each other for economic supremacy, taxing each other's goods and otherwise refusing to trade freely among themselves. The federal government, lacking executive and judicial power and possessing only a weak legislature, couldn't do anything to preserve interstate harmony. When the Constitutional Convention met in 1787, it was clear that the federal government needed to be given more power, but a lot of disagreement remained between the so-called federalists and anti-federalists about exactly how much.

In many ways, the Constitution represents a compromise between these two camps. Most importantly, although the Constitution creates a substantial, three-branch national government, it confers upon that government only a series of specific, limited powers; everything else is left to the states. As discussed in chapter 2, Congress may only exercise those powers enumerated by the Constitution; the founding document does not give Congress any sort of general police power to regulate purely local activities. Likewise, as discussed in chapter 4, the jurisdiction of the federal judiciary is limited to cases involving federal law and cases involving plaintiffs and defendants from different states. Run-of-the-mill controversies about real property, contract terms, criminal law, and negligently dropping a brick on someone's foot generally cannot be heard by the federal courts.

In addition, two key amendments to the Constitution specifically protect the states. The Eleventh Amendment, ratified in 1795, says: "The Judicial power of the United States shall not be construed to extend to any suit in law or equity, commenced or prosecuted against one of the United States by Citizens of another State, or by Citizens or Subjects of any Foreign State." The amendment was motivated by a famous early Supreme Court case called *Chisholm v. Georgia,* which held that a citizen of South Carolina could sue the State of Georgia to recover debts from the Revolutionary War. The states kind of freaked out about the idea that people could sue them for the mountains of debt they had incurred during the war, and they acted promptly to enact the Eleventh Amendment. Even though the language of the amendment clearly does not bar citizens from suing their own state and clearly applies only to federal courts, the Supreme Court has priggishly extended the amendment to all citizens and all courts. As a result, states are immune from a lot of lawsuits that they shouldn't be, like suits brought against them by their own citizens to enforce federal employment or environmental laws, even if these suits are brought in state court.

Then there's the Tenth Amendment. This curious little number—the final entry in the Bill of Rights, ratified in 1791—says that "[t]he powers not delegated to the United States by the Constitution, nor prohibited by it to the States, are reserved to the States respectively, or to the people." It's unclear what this is supposed to mean. On the one hand, there's a good argument that it does nothing but remind everyone that if the Constitution doesn't give a power to the federal government, then that power continues to reside with the states. On the other hand, it does seem strange that the framers would create a whole constitutional amendment to serve as nothing more than an FYI Post it note. Accordingly, the Supreme Court has from time to time used the Tenth Amendment to strike down federal laws that order or "commandeer" the states to carry out some federal requirement, like the time Congress ordered every state to come up with a plan to dispose of all hazardous waste within their borders or else take ownership of the waste, or when the Brady Bill required state officials to do background checks on anyone seeking to buy a gun. It is worth noting, however, that nothing in the Tenth Amendment stops the federal government from basically coercing the states by threatening to take funds away from them if they don't do what the feds want.

Although the Constitution gives the states a lot of latitude to do as they wish, it also places a number of specific limits on the little guys. For one thing, there's the supremacy clause of Article VI, which says that federal law is the "supreme Law of the Land." This clause makes it clear that if a federal law and a state law conflict, the federal law trumps. That's why, for example, it's still technically illegal to use marijuana for medical purposes in California. Second, Article I, Section 10, of the Constitution lays out a series of specific limits on the states—they are forbidden, for instance, from issuing titles of nobility (see chapter 8), keeping troops, engaging in war with foreign nations, or coining their own money. Moreover, most of the Bill of Rights, including the rights to free speech, freedom of religion, and freedom from unreasonable searches and seizures, has also been applied by the Supreme Court to the states by way of the due process clause of the Fourteenth Amendment.

Finally, one of the most important restrictions on state power is one that doesn't seem to actually be in the Constitution, at least explicitly. As I mentioned in the last chapter, the Supreme Court has long interpreted Article I, Section 8's commerce clause—the provision that gives Congress the power to regulate interstate commerce—as implicitly restricting the states from regulating interstate commerce themselves. The Court has used what's bizarrely been referred to as the "dormant commerce clause" to solve the major problem haunting the Republic under the Articles of Confederation—states passing laws to protect their own local economies—and to ensure the existence of a true national economy with a free flow of goods across state lines. Under the dormant commerce clause, any state law that facially discriminates against out-of-state goods by banning them or taxing them or whatever is unconstitutional unless Congress

has specifically authorized such a law or the law is necessary to protect some compelling state interest unrelated to
protecting its economy. This last exception is quite narrow.
Only once—when Maine banned the import of live baitfish
to protect its "fragile fisheries"—has the Supreme Court upheld a discriminatory state law on that basis, and that was
because baitfish from outside Maine had some nasty parasite
that Maine baitfish generally didn't have.

I would bet that most average twenty-first-century Americans, if you asked them, would say that it's really weird that
two out of the twenty-seven amendments in the Constitution have to do with booze. Why would our most important
legal document single out something so mundane and pe-
destrian as alcoholic beverages, of all things? Drinking alcohol to excess is obviously unhealthy, and its secondary effects,
like drunk driving and violence, are worth some bits of federal or state legislation here and there, but two constitutional
amendments? For real?

To understand how prohibiting the manufacture and sale
of alcoholic beverages could have become a matter of constitutional concern requires some creative imagination of how
Americans in the late nineteenth and early twentieth centuries viewed booze and its associated problems. For many
abstainers, or "drys," in this period, alcohol was pure evil.
Remember, Americans (mostly men) drank a *lot* back then,
and when they drank, it was often in male-only saloons.
This was not an era, in other words, when men and women
sipped gin and tonics together by the pool or went club hop-
ping arm-in-arm after work. Men would disappear with the
week's wages and blow it in the saloons on drinks and pros-
titutes, leaving their wives and children at home, scrounging
for food until the husbands showed up sometimes days later

to give them all a good beating. As Daniel Okrent, author of the superb book *Last Call: The Rise and Fall of Prohibition*, puts it: "Saloons were dark and nasty places, and to the wives of the men inside, they were satanic."

Put this situation together with the fact that alcohol was often identified with European immigrants and racial minorities, and it starts to make sense that groups of nativists, racists, and women's rights activists could come together in various unlikely alliances to convince a slew of states to prohibit or restrict the manufacture and sale of alcohol within their borders. Here, however, a strange early quirk of the dormant commerce clause came into play. Back in the early twentieth century, under the Supreme Court's so-called "original package" doctrine, states were not allowed to regulate the sale of products coming from other states within their own borders so long as the product remained in its original package. This led to the counterintuitive result that states could not prohibit saloons from selling liquor imported from other states. To remedy this problem, Congress passed the Webb-Kenyon Act, which, in language very similar to what would become Section 2 of the Twenty-first Amendment, made it a federal crime to ship intoxicating liquor from one state to another state in violation of the latter state's laws.

Although Webb-Kenyon closed one of the major loopholes that had made liquor regulation on the state level problematic, many hard-core drys were still unsatisfied with the patchwork of state laws regarding alcohol. Not all states banned liquor, and those that did varied in how strict they were about it. When the Sixteenth Amendment reversed an earlier Supreme Court decision and made it legal for the government to institute an income tax—thus substantially reducing the fiscal need to tax liquor—and World War I brought German breweries like Anheuser-Busch into disrepute—the stage was finally set for the drys to prevail in their long-standing battle to put Prohibition in the Constitution. And, thus, Section 1 of the Eighteenth Amendment: "After one year from the ratification of this article the manufacture, sale, or transportation of intoxicating liquors within, the importation thereof into, or the exportation thereof from the United States and all territory subject to the jurisdiction thereof for beverage purposes is hereby prohibited."

The text of the amendment left a number of questions unanswered—such as, for instance, what counts as an "intoxicating liquor"—so Congress filled these gaps through a statute called the Volstead Act. The act defined the key word "intoxicating" to include anything one could ingest that contained more than 0.5 percent alcohol, which, as Okrent points out, technically made it illegal to sell sauerkraut and German chocolate cake, as well as the least alcoholic of beers and wines. The act also came up with a few interesting exceptions. For example, the statute made it legal for rich people to drink in their own homes any alcohol purchased before the effective date of the Eighteenth Amendment (the act didn't actually explicitly limit this exception to "rich people," but who else had stockpiled liquor in their basements?). The act exempted sacramental wine, which was nice, since it meant that Catholics and Jews could continue to practice their religions, as well as cider and fermented fruit juices, which was also nice, since it meant that (again, according to Okrent) "no husbandman would be denied the barrel by the homestead door, the jug stashed in a corner of the field, the comforting warmth on cold country nights."

Prohibition, naturally, was a complete disaster. Organized crime flourished. Corruption thrived. Violence blossomed. Poisoning from crudely distilled alcohol became rampant. Federal anticrime forces were overwhelmed (Section 2 of the Eighteenth Amendment provided that both the feds and the states had jurisdiction over its enforcement). And still people drank nearly as much as they had before, though in different ways and in various degrees of secrecy. Once again, larger forces appeared on the scene, and when the Great Depression made the absurdity of prohibiting booze on a federal level inescapably obvious, the country's "wets" were able to secure passage of the Twenty-first Amendment, Section 1, of which provided: "The eighteenth article of amendment to the Constitution of the United States is hereby repealed."

Section 1 of the Twenty-first Amendment is clear as a bell, but what about Section 2? *The Transportation or importation into any State, Territory, or Possession of the United States for delivery or use therein of intoxicating liquors, in violation of the laws thereof, is hereby prohibited.* Probably the oddest thing about this section is that it directly regulates the behavior of private parties rather than the government. Every other provision in the Constitution, except for one, tells the government what it can or must or cannot do. If you haven't thought about this before, you might want to find the Constitution online and skim through it (we thought about reprinting it as an appendix at the end of the book, but that would have added $1 to the price of the book; *you're welcome*). Notice how just about *never* does the Constitution place any limit on individuals or other private actors like associations or corporations or religious groups or anyone else. The only two exceptions are Section 2 of the Twenty-first Amendment and Section 1 of the Thirteenth Amendment, which prohibits slavery. This unique feature of the Twenty-first Amendment led Harvard professor Laurence Tribe, probably the preeminent scholar on the US Constitution, to nominate Section 2 as the Constitution's stupidest clause. As Tribe puts it:

[T]here are two ways, and two ways only, in which an ordinary private citizen, acting under her own steam and color of no law, can violate the United

States Constitution. One is to enslave somebody, a suitably hellish act. The other is to bring a bottle of beer, wine, or bourbon into a State in violation of its beverage control laws—an act that might have been thought juvenile, and perhaps even lawless, but *unconstitutional?*

Beyond this quirk, however, it remains unclear what exactly the framers of Section 2 were attempting to accomplish. There are two basic theories of what's going on with the clause—what experts have called the "maximalist" and the "minimalist" theories, although of course there are intermediate positions as well. According to the maximalist theory, Section 2 gives the states complete power to regulate liquor, including the power to pass laws that would otherwise violate earlier-enacted provisions of the Constitution, including the First Amendment and the dormant commerce clause. On the other hand, defenders of a more minimalist approach to the clause say that it's merely meant to constitutionalize the Webb-Kenyon Act and make clear that states may regulate alcohol coming from outside their borders, so long as that regulation otherwise comports with the rest of the Constitution.

The Supreme Court has struggled to make sense of Section 2 almost since it first became law. Early on, the Court took a fairly maximalist stance. In 1936, in a case called *State Board of Equalization of California v. Young's Market Co.,* the Court heard a challenge to a California law that charged $500 to import beer for sale into the state. California storeowners who wanted to import beer from companies in Wisconsin and Missouri argued that the law violated the dormant commerce clause because it discriminated against out-of-state beer enterprises. The Supreme Court conceded that absent the Twenty-first Amendment, the law would surely have been unconstitutional. Section 2, however, saved the day for California. The Court couldn't have been clearer in saying that Section 2 basically gave California carte blanche to do whatever it wanted with liquor. "The words used are apt to confer upon the state the power to forbid all importations which do not comply with the conditions which it prescribes," wrote the Court. It continued: "The plaintiffs ask us to limit this broad command. They request us to construe the amendment as saying, in effect: The state may prohibit the importation of intoxicating liquors provided it prohibits the manufacture and sale within its borders; but if it permits such manufacture and sale, it must let imported liquors compete with the domestic on equal terms. To say that, would involve not a construction of the amendment, but a rewriting of it." In response to the out-of-state beer companies' alternative argument that California's law violated their Fourteenth Amendment equal protection rights, the Court was even more succinct: "A classification recognized by the Twenty-first Amendment cannot be deemed forbidden by the Fourteenth."

In the years following *Young's Market,* the Court softened its position a little bit on Section 2, but it continued to find that the Twenty-first Amendment often allowed states to pass laws about booze that they couldn't have otherwise passed. In the bottomless-dancing vagina-dollar-bill-picking-up case (*California v. LaRue*) that I described at the beginning of the chapter, for instance, the Court stopped short of saying that the First Amendment was irrelevant, but it did nonetheless uphold a law that was questionable under free speech principles, saying that it wouldn't "insist that the sort of bacchanalian revelries that the Department sought to prevent by these liquor regulations were the constitutional equivalent of a performance by a scantily clad ballet troupe in a theater." Ten years later, the Court extended this line of reasoning up above the waist when in a case called *N.Y. State Liquor Authority v. Bellanca,* it upheld a New York law banning topless dancing in establishments holding liquor licenses. "Whatever artistic or communicative value may attach to topless dancing," the Court said, "is overcome by the State's exercise of its broad powers arising under the Twenty-first Amendment."

More recently, however, the Supreme Court has retreated from this maximalist position when it comes to whether the states may ignore the First Amendment, Fourteenth Amendment, and other constitutional provisions protecting individual liberties. For example, in *Craig v. Boren,* the Court struck down an Oklahoma law saying that people without Y chromosomes could buy 3.2 percent beer when they turned eighteen, while people with Y chromosomes had to wait until they turned twenty-one. The Court said this was a violation of men's equal protection rights and that the Twenty-first Amendment was irrelevant. Likewise, in a case called *44 Liquormart Inc. v. Rhode Island,* the Court reiterated the irrelevance of the Twenty-first Amendment in a free speech case involving liquor advertising. Both cases basically said that the California bottomless-dancing decision was no longer good law, though the Court was also careful enough to say that the government can still regulate nude dancing because, well, it didn't give any good reason but basically we can assume that the Court just thinks nude dancing is depraved and disgusting.

Nevertheless, once in a while you do see a case from a lower court that relies on Section 2 of the Twenty-first Amendment to uphold some state or local regulation about alcohol. When the city of San Juan, Puerto Rico, for instance, passed an ordinance in 2004 banning alcohol sales between midnight and 7:00 a.m. in certain areas of the city to reduce crime, noise, garbage, and abandoned vehicles, a federal district court cited the government's "heightened authority under the Twenty First Amendment" in support of its decision to uphold the law. Section 2 also played a role in a fabulous case from Springfield, Missouri, called *Spudich v. Smarr.* The State of Missouri allowed "amusement places" to apply for liquor licenses, with the term "amusement places" defined as buildings of a certain size "where games of skill commonly known as bowling or soccer are usually played." A guy named Spudich, who owned a pool hall in town, applied for a liquor license and was denied, since nobody played "bowling or soccer" in his pool hall. Spudich claimed the law was irrational, but a federal appellate court disagreed. One the one hand, the court thought that the Missouri legislature "could have believed that billiard parlors . . . represented a greater threat of disruptive behavior" because playing pool has a slower pace and requires less physical exertion than bowling or soccer. On the other hand, the court hypothesized that maybe soccer and bowling establishments were more family-friendly places than pool halls and thus could benefit from a little booze: "The legislature may reasonably have believed," said the judges, "that allowing the sale of liquor at certain family-oriented sports facilities, such as bowling alleys and soccer stadiums, would provide a relaxing atmosphere that would enhance the recreational aspect of the day." In finding the state law constitutional, the court relied on its view that under Section 2 of the Twenty-first Amendment, "There is an added presumption in favor of the validity of state regulation in the area of liquor control."

Given the Court's holdings in *Craig v. Boren* and *44 Liquormart,* these lower-court decisions breathing life into Section 2 seem a little misguided. Still, though, at least one scholar believes it makes sense to read Section 2 as giving states additional powers to prohibit liquor-related activities that cause harms mirroring the harms that existed prior to Prohibition. Marcia Yablon-Zug, a professor at University of South Carolina Law School, has argued that despite Prohibition's failure, the temperance movement that brought about Prohibition had pursued a number of worthwhile goals—

including reducing the harms of the saloon culture that per-
vaded American life in the early twentieth century—that
remained important even when it became clear that Prohibition, as a whole, was not working. Yablon-Zug argues that
Section 2 was "created to effectuate these temperance goals."
Supporting the decision in *Spudich,* for example, Yablon-
Zug cites a bunch of cases and newspaper articles that show
"the continued seediness of pool halls" and concludes that
"pool halls are rarely family establishments, and many have
the same undesirable qualities as the old saloon." If pool
halls and bottomless-dancing clubs are just new manifesta-
tions of the pre-Prohibition culture of male-only drinking,
violence, and prostitution, then by all means, Yablon-Zug
suggests, states should be able to regulate them to protect
the families that are the victims of this culture. Viewed this
way, the Twenty-first Amendment wasn't about giving alcohol the green light at all; rather, it was about taking the
power to prohibit and regulate alcohol away from the federal government and giving that power—in a highly robust
form—back to the states.

States regulate alcohol in strict and complicated ways. When
it comes to distribution, they generally use some version of
a three-tiered system that separates producers, distributors,
and retailers. This is why it's not always that easy to just go
to the Web site of your favorite Paso Robles or Willamette
Valley winery and order up a case of their best pinot noir
shipped to your door. On the other hand, the growth of the
Internet and the rise of smaller wineries have placed a lot of
pressure on state legislatures to loosen their grip on direct
wine sales to consumers. As a result, many states have started
to allow these direct shipments, although the specifics of
what's allowed and what isn't differ a lot by state. For a while,

around the turn of the millennium, some states started allowing in-state wineries to sell directly to consumers but not out-of-state wineries. For instance, Michigan required wine producers generally to go through wholesalers, except for the forty or so Michigan wineries, which could purchase a fairly cheap "wine maker" license that allowed them to sell directly to Michigan buyers. New York did basically the same thing, although it allowed out-of-state wineries to sell directly to New York consumers if they set up a "branch factory, office, or storeroom" within New York, something no out-of-state winery had any intention of doing.

In 2004 dormant-commerce-clause challenges to both of these discriminatory state laws made it to the Supreme Court, in *Granholm v. Heald.* Some of the biggest lawyers around were involved in the case, from Kenneth Starr, who almost ruined the country, to Robert Bork, who would have ruined the country if he had been confirmed to the Supreme Court, to Eliot Spitzer, who allegedly had sex with whores. All eyes were watching, from state regulators to the wine industry to underage college freshmen with Internet connections, credit cards, and a hankering for some top-end sauvignon blanc with notes of grapefruit, pepperoncini, and cat litter.

The Court decided 5–4 that the state regulations were unconstitutional. The lineup of justices was just about as odd as the Twenty-first Amendment itself. Rather than explaining what the various justices thought about the case, though, I figured it would be more fun if I presented their deliberations in a little play, which I call *The Justices Deliberate* Granholm v. Heald:

The justices sit around their giant conference table eating lunch and discussing how to decide the case.

JUSTICE STEVENS: Well, I think that these state regulations are fine. Alcohol is not the same as any other product. I mean, we have not one but two constitutional amendments about the hooch. The Twenty-first Amendment might have repealed Prohibition, but Section 2 "gave the States the option to maintain equally comprehensive prohibitions in their respective jurisdictions."

JUSTICE THOMAS: I agree with Justice Stevens.

JUSTICE STEVENS: You do? Really? When was the last time we agreed?

JUSTICE THOMAS: I don't know. Didn't we agree back in 1992 that we both enjoyed *A Few Good Men*? Anyway, look at the *Young's Market* case from 1936. We said it was fine for California to tax beer imports from outside the state because Section 2 trumps the dormant commerce clause.

JUSTICE SCALIA: What? I totally disagree. Have you guys read our more recent cases? The 3.2 percent beer case? The *44 Liquormart* case? Your cases are yesterday's newspaper. The newer cases have basically held that the Twenty-first Amendment doesn't do jack.

JUSTICE SOUTER: I can't believe I'm saying this, but I think Scalia's right. Remember the *Bacchus Imports v. Dias* case from 1984?

JUSTICE O'CONNOR: Isn't that the one where Hawaii had imposed a 20 percent tax on all wholesale liquor sales but had exempted locally made pineapple wine and an indigenous-shrub-based brandy called okolehao from the tax? We said that the tax violated the dormant commerce clause even though sales of okolehao and pineapple wine made up no more than 0.7739 percent of total liquor sales in any given year.

JUSTICE REHNQUIST: Mmmmm, pineapple wine. Yummy.

JUSTICE BREYER: I bet a cup of okolehao would pair nicely with this turkey and muenster sandwich I'm eating.

JUSTICE SCALIA: You've got turkey? Want to trade? I've got peanut butter and banana.

JUSTICE BREYER: No way you're getting any of my turkey. I'll give you my cookie for your brownie, though.

JUSTICE GINSBURG: Can we focus here, people? Jeez!

JUSTICE SOUTER: Thank you, Justice Ginsburg. As Nino and I were saying, our most recent cases, including the Hawaii case, have very clearly held that Section 2 does not authorize states to violate the strict dictates of the dormant commerce clause. That's exactly what Michigan and New York have done here, so I say we strike down the challenged laws.

JUSTICE STEVENS: I vociferously disagree. You whipper-snappers might be under eighty-three years old, but I'm not, and I remember well what Prohibition was about. The people who wrote the Twenty-first Amendment meant to give the states the power to regulate alcohol however they want. The justices who decided our early cases on this matter, like *Young's Market,* had lived through the 1920s and understood this. We should respect the original meaning of the amendment.

JUSTICE THOMAS *[giggling under his breath]:* Stevens is so old.

JUSTICE REHNQUIST: What about this argument the states make that banning direct sales from out-of-state wineries is necessary to discourage underage drinking? They say it's just like the Maine baitfish case.

JUSTICE GINSBURG: No, that's ridiculous. Kids can't wait eight seconds between checking their text messages. They're not going to order wine over the Internet and wait three days to get it.

JUSTICE O'CONNOR *[leaning toward Justice Rehnquist and whispering]:* What does Ginsburg know about text messaging?

JUSTICE BREYER: Plus, the states exempt in-state wineries from the no-direct-sales rule anyway. This totally undermines their whole argument. If a kid from East Lansing or Ann Arbor wants to get hammered on wine, some northern Michigan swill will do just as well as Napa Valley Opus One.

JUSTICE SCALIA: I never thought I'd say this, but I'm with Ginsburg, Breyer, and Souter on this one. Yikes. I better go have my head examined. Does anyone have a gavel I can bite in half?

JUSTICE THOMAS: Well, it looks like Rehnquist, O'Connor, and Stevens are on my side. We've heard from everyone except Justice Kennedy. It's 4–4, Anthony. I guess it's up to you.

EVERYONE ON THE COURT OTHER THAN JUSTICE KENNEDY: *Again!*

Justice Kennedy takes off his headphones and turns off the portable television he was watching, which was turned to The Jeffersons.

JUSTICE KENNEDY: Oh, is it time for me to make the law for the land now? I agree with Scalia. Our newer cases trump the older ones. I say the laws are unconstitutional.

JUSTICES SCALIA, SOUTER, GINSBURG, AND BREYER: Yippee.

JUSTICE STEVENS: Why do I even bother showing up here anymore?

∽

The question of how much power the states should have in the federal system was a primary concern of the Constitution's framers, and it remains a big deal today. In the past twenty or so years, the Supreme Court's so-called New Federalism approach to issues involving state power, like whether the commerce clause places significant constraints on congressional power and how broad state immunity from suit should be under the Eleventh Amendment, has resulted in states having a bit more power and freedom than in some earlier periods. But the federal government remains extremely powerful, and the idea that the Supreme Court will ever put truly significant restrictions on federal power seems unlikely.

The puzzle of Section 2 of the Twenty-first Amendment is one part of this state-power question, and it is interesting that, by cutting down in recent years on the amount of power Section 2 offers states to regulate liquor, the Court has gone against its general trend of finding in favor of state power. What's more interesting, though, is what the Court's approach to Section 2 tells us about constitutional interpretation generally. One of the hard questions when it comes to interpreting the Constitution is whether judges should interpret provisions differently as social and cultural attitudes toward various things—sex, drugs, religion, technology, race, gender, etc., etc.—change over time. Some say yes, the Constitution should be read as a "living document" so that it continues to remain relevant to our current situation, while others say that unelected judges have no authority to change the Constitution's meaning and that the document's original meaning must endure, at least until it's formally amended.

In most cases, it can be difficult to get a handle on this disjunction between original meaning and current conditions, because most of the Constitution is well over two hundred years old, and even some of the more important amendments, like the Fourteenth, have been around for nearly a century and a half. It's not easy to imagine how the framers, writing in the late eighteenth century, for instance, would have thought about funding public Jewish schools or regulating Internet porn or legalizing gay marriage. The disconnect is just too overwhelming. But with the drosophila-fruit-fly-like Section 2, now only about seventy-five years old, the issue is more accessible. We generally feel differently about liquor now than we did in the mid-1930s, but it's not so difficult to put ourselves into the shoes of those who struggled with Prohibition, and this makes it easier to think about whether we should interpret the Constitution dynamically. If you think the liberal Justice Stevens is right about the meaning of Section 2, doesn't that mean you believe that the Constitution's original meaning should prevail? If you think that the more conservative justices Kennedy and Scalia are right, doesn't that mean you believe the Constitution should be a living document?

Maybe, maybe not. But the next time you find yourself in a seedy pool hall watching a bottomless-dance routine while enjoying a tall frosty mug of pineapple wine, it might be worth thinking about.

CHAPTER 7

The Letters of Marque and Reprisal Clause

Foreign Affairs

> The Congress shall have Power to . . . grant Letters of Marque and Reprisal.
>
> *Article I, Section 8*

Americans adore pirates! We dress up like pirates on Halloween and bellow "Arrrr, matey!" at our friends and feed imaginary treats to the invisible parrots perched on our shoulders. We spend every September 19 celebrating International Talk Like a Pirate Day and occasionally change our Facebook language settings to pirate mode (yes, this is a real thing). But despite their curiously romantic appeal, pirates actually suck. They sucked back in the seventeenth and eighteenth centuries when they lawlessly plundered innocent ships with cannons and swords, and they continue to suck today, as they use their high-tech GPS equipment and automatic weapons to wreak havoc along the Horn of Africa and elsewhere.

In April of 2009, the *Maersk Alabama,* a huge unarmed American cargo ship carrying food for various international relief organizations, was on its way from Djibouti to Kenya when four Somali pirates attacked it, seized Richard Phillips, the *Alabama*'s captain, and demanded millions of dollars in ransom. Naval officers on the USS *Bainbridge,* a destroyer that had been patrolling the Indian Ocean at the time of the attack, negotiated for days with the terrorists, but to no avail. When the lifeboat the pirates were in ran out of fuel, they accepted the *Bainbridge*'s offer to tow them a short way behind the American warship. In the meantime, a crack team of Navy SEAL snipers had been flown to the area, where they parachuted into the sea and were brought aboard the *Bainbridge.* Tensions had been high for days, with the pirates repeatedly threatening to kill the captain, but when a bullet was fired aboard the lifeboat sometime near dusk on April 12, President Obama gave the go-ahead for the snipers to start sniping. The Navy marksmen donned night-vision glasses and waited for exactly the right moment. When two of the pirates stuck their heads out of the lifeboat's rear hatch, and the third remaining pirate became visible through a window at the bow of the boat, the three SEALs fired. Rescuers from the *Bainbridge* boarded the lifeboat and found all the pirates dead. Captain Phillips was rescued, basically unharmed. Amazingly, the SEALs had fired only three bullets to end the crisis.

In the wake of the affair, there was of course much celebrating the heroism of both Captain Phillips and the Navy SEALs, but this cheering was accompanied by debates over what to do about the increasing problem of Somali pirates. The naval operation that ended the *Alabama* crisis had allegedly cost tens of millions of dollars. Might there be some better and cheaper way to fight these pesky pirates? Among the recommendations came a curious one from the always controversial, libertarian-leaning Republican congressman from Texas, Ron Paul. Representative Paul suggested that perhaps the government could authorize private vessels to fight pirates in return for bounty money. That way, the US government could use the market, rather than its own fire-power, to solve the piracy problem. As one supporter of the proposal observed, "If we have 100 American wannabe Rambos patrolling the seas, it's probably a good way of getting the job done."

But wait, would this solution be constitutional? Can the US government actually contract out its key naval functions? Representative Paul certainly thought so. Following Paul's proposal, the government would use its power under Article I of the Constitution to grant "letters of marque and reprisal" to private vessels; these letters would authorize the private ships to fight pirates on the government's behalf. If this seems like kind of an antiquated solution to you, well, it is. The United States hasn't issued a letter of marque or reprisal in almost two hundred years.

The big constitutional question when it comes to foreign affairs is who, as between the Congress and the president, has the power to do what. The place to start is the text of the Constitution, which allocates various foreign affairs powers between the two branches. The president has the power to enter into treaties with foreign nations, subject to Senate confirmation. The president also has the power to "receive Ambassadors and other public Ministers." Most importantly, Article II, Section 2, of the Constitution makes the president the "Commander in Chief of the Army and Navy of the United States." On the other hand, Article I of the Constitution gives Congress the power to "declare War," "raise and support Armies," "provide and maintain a Navy," and "make Rules for the Government and Regulation of the land and Naval Forces." Congress is also given a bunch of pirate-y powers, including not only the marque and reprisal power, but also the authority to "make Rules concerning Captures on Land and Water" and "to define and punish Piracies and Felonies committed on the high Seas."

All told, there aren't that many words in the Constitution about foreign affairs, but the commentary that these few words have engendered could fill the main branch of a midsize US city's public library. Two issues have captured most of the attention. The first issue is whether (and to what extent) the president can instigate hostilities short of a declared war without congressional approval, apart from acting in an emergency to repel a sudden attack (which everyone agrees the president can do). The second issue is whether (and to what extent) Congress can limit or control the scope of the president's power once war or other hostilities have begun. The first question was the big one during the whole Vietnam War fiasco; the second question has risen to the forefront as a result of more recent fiascos.

Another way of putting the first issue is like this: Can the president start what looks like a war even though Congress has not declared war? As it turns out, although the United States has engaged in hostilities with foreign nations over a hundred discrete times in our history, Congress has only issued a formal declaration of war five times: during the War of 1812, the Mexican-American War, the Spanish-American War, and the two world wars. Operation Iraqi Freedom? The Gulf War? Vietnam? Korea? All undeclared, to say nothing of our many smaller, presidentially initiated hostile operations, like our relatively recent interventions in Haiti, Somalia, and Bosnia. Were these undeclared warlike things constitutionally illegitimate?

A lot of legal and policy commentators think that at least some of them were. Their view is that while the "commander in chief clause" may give the president wide latitude to make tactical decisions about how to prosecute hostilities once they've begun, the Constitution gives Congress the exclusive power to decide whether to start these hostilities in the first place. For example, the late John Hart Ely, dean of the Stanford Law School in the 1980s and probably on most legal academics' top-ten list of all-time-greatest constitutional scholars, once argued that while the "original understanding" of many parts of the Constitution "can be obscure to the point of inscrutability," this is not the case with the Constitution's allocation of war powers: "The power to declare war was constitutionally vested in Congress. The debates, and early practice, establish that this meant that all wars, big or small, 'declared' in so many words or not—most weren't, even then—had to be legislatively authorized." In the words of another pro-Congress scholar, "The constitutional framework adopted by the framers is clear in its basic principles. The authority to initiate war lay with Congress. The President could act unilaterally only in one area: to repel sudden attacks. Anyone who scans the war-power provisions of the Constitution is likely to agree . . . that 'the text tilts decisively toward Congress.'" These scholars unsurprisingly also believe that it's better for Congress to have the exclusive power to initiate hostilities, because as a large deliberative body, it is less likely to impetuously involve the nation in some sort of military morass than a single person.

On the other hand, a good number of presidential-power hawks have argued that the president's power to instigate hostilities is far greater than these stingy pro-Congress scholars would admit. These scholars tend to argue that the "declare war clause" grants Congress only the power to formally recognize that a state of war exists between the United States and a foreign country, and that the clause has nothing to do with the decision to start hostilities. Why then have such a seemingly unimportant clause? In the words of Professor John Yoo of the University of California at Berkeley, one of the authors of the "torture memo" (to which we will return shortly), the "primary function" of a congressional declaration of war "was to trigger the international laws of war, which would clothe in legitimacy certain actions taken against one's own and enemy citizens." Once the declare war clause is put aside as a source of the power to instigate hostilities, the commander in chief clause, combined with a long history of presidential hostility-initiation going back to the eighteenth century, are left as strong evidence that the framers intended the president to be able to start wars without congressional authorization. Once again, shockingly, the policy preferences of these scholars align perfectly with their reading of the constitutional text and the nation's history. Having a single person in charge of the decision to go to war ensures, in their view, that the government is directly accountable to the electorate and that it can (in Yoo's words) act "swiftly and with decisiveness" in the face of external dangers.

This disagreement over war powers came to a head during the Vietnam War, as Presidents Lyndon Johnson and Richard Nixon continued to pour money and troops into the conflict without an existing formal congressional declaration of war. Congress responded in 1973 by passing (over a presidential veto) a law called the War Powers Resolution. The resolution provides that the president can only send troops into hostilities in an emergency or when Congress has either declared war or authorized the president's action by statute. The president must then withdraw the troops after sixty days unless Congress has officially declared war by that point. The resolution is symbolically interesting but, as a practical matter, largely irrelevant. Pretty much all the presidents who have served since 1973 believe the War Powers Resolution unconstitutionally limits the president's power to initiate hostilities under the commander in chief clause, and, despite the fact that presidents have uniformly ignored the resolution, Congress has not insisted that these presidents follow it. The Supreme Court, for its part, has routinely refused to consider challenges to the president's decision to initiate hostilities, generally invoking the so-called political-question doctrine, which is basically something the Court has come up with so it can dodge issues it deems too politically dicey for courts to get anywhere near.

The second big constitutional foreign affairs issue has to do with the scope of the president's powers to conduct a war once the country is in one. Does the commander in chief power give the president the exclusive authority to make decisions about how the war is to be carried out—decisions, for instance, about tactics, manpower, or treatment of prisoners—or does Congress also possess some power, by virtue of its constitutional authority to support and make rules for the armed forces, to decide some of these things itself?

The question became particularly important during the administration of George W. Bush, when it emerged that the administration's plans for "enhanced interrogation" (that's a Bushism for "torture") would potentially violate a congressional statute making it illegal for anyone to "commit or attempt to commit torture." In an August 1, 2002, memorandum sent by Jay Bybee, the head of the Office of Legal Counsel at the Justice Department (and now—yikes!—a federal appellate judge), to White House counsel Alberto Gonzalez, the Justice Department not only interpreted the statute's definition of torture incredibly narrowly, but it also argued that to the extent the statute might ban some useful instances of torture, the law would violate the president's authority to conduct war. The memo was drafted primarily by the aforementioned John Yoo, and it expressed a sweeping view of the president's commander in chief power. As the memo puts it, "the President enjoys complete discretion in the exercise of his Commander-in-Chief authority and in conducting operations against hostile forces." As a result, the antitorture statute would have to bend. The memo concludes:

As Commander-in-Chief, the President has the constitutional authority to order interrogations of enemy
combatants to gain intelligence information concerning the military plans of the enemy. The demands of
the Commander-in-Chief power are especially pronounced in the middle of a war in which the nation
has already suffered a direct attack. In such a case, the
information gained from interrogations may prevent
future attacks by foreign enemies. Any effort to apply
[the antitorture statute] in a manner that interferes
with the President's direction of such core war matters
as the detention and interrogation of enemy combatants thus would be unconstitutional.

The torture memo, when it was released, proved to be
controversial, to put it mildly. More accurately, people went
nuts. Harold Koh, for one—the Yale Law School dean at
the time and also a former and future bigwig legal adviser
in the State Department—called it "the most clearly legally
erroneous opinion I have ever read." The subsequent head of
OLC in the Bush administration withdrew the opinion, and
the Obama administration completely repudiated it. Official
investigations into wrongdoing on the part of the memo's
authors were conducted. Spain has considered indicting six
Bush administration officials, including Bybee and Yoo, on
war crimes charges.

Meanwhile, scholars have started looking more carefully
into the question of how much power over war-making decisions the commander in chief clause actually gives to the
president and leaves to the Congress. These scholars have
examined the early practices of the Republic to see whether
Congress in fact made tactical and operational decisions
regarding war during the time of the framers, as a way of
trying to understand what the Constitution's drafters intended. One dynamic duo of scholars from Harvard and

Georgetown (who both incidentally took high-up positions at OLC in the Obama administration) concluded that "there is surprisingly little Founding-era evidence supporting the notion that the conduct of military campaigns is beyond legislative control and a fair amount of evidence that affirmatively undermines it." Professor Prakash of the University of Virginia, whom we met earlier in connection with the question of whether someone can be a senator and the president at the same time, basically concurs. Noting that early Congresses not only "regulated the treatment of enemy prisoners" but also made such down-in-the-trenches decisions as where "warships might sail in wartime" and "how soldiers would march and fire arms," Prakash concludes that "the Constitution creates a powerful Commander-in-Chief who is authorized to direct military operations, but who is nevertheless subject to congressional direction in all war and military matters."

In the midst of this new concern over whether Congress can make decisions about how wars should be carried out, scholars have turned to the letters of marque and reprisal clause to see whether it might shed any light on the question. In a way, this might seem sort of surprising—what could a clause dealing with the authorization of privateers to fight pirates have to do with whether Congress can regulate the president's power to interrogate prisoners?—but on the other hand, perhaps it's quite natural. After all, scholars have been talking about the letters of marque and reprisal clause in connection with the first constitutional foreign affairs question (the one about initiating hostilities) ever since the Vietnam War.

English kings and other European rulers had authorized private ships to attack foreign vessels as far back as the fourteenth century. Back then, different terms were used for different kinds of authorizations—for those granted during wartime, for those granted during peace, for those granted to private individuals who had themselves been wronged somehow by a foreign state, and so on. Some of the authorizations were called "letters of marque" and some were called "letters of reprisal," and there were other names as well. By the eighteenth century, however, all these nomenclature distinctions seem to have disappeared, and a "letter of marque and reprisal" came to refer to any authorization from a government to a private vessel to attack a foreign ship and take its stuff. A ship sailing with a letter of marque could attack a foreign ship without violating international law; absent the letter of marque, the same attack would constitute piracy, typically punishable by death. Letters of marque included specific conditions that the private vessel had to follow if its owners wanted to keep their booty. So-called prize courts existed to adjudicate claims among vessels that some particular booty had not been properly bootified and was therefore not bootylicious (note: not official legal terms).

Letters of marque and reprisal played an important role for the American colonies during the Revolution. The colonies didn't have a lot of money, and they didn't have much of an organized navy, so they had to rely heavily on private vessels to fight their sea battles and capture British ships. According to one estimate, the colonial government had a total of sixty-four ships in its navy, but it issued almost eight hundred letters of marque and reprisal to privateers. These private vessels captured three times the number of British ships captured by the actual navy. In the War of 1812, the imbalance between naval ships and ships sailing under letters of marque and reprisal was even greater. Only twenty-two ships sailed for the American Navy, while several hundred private ships sailed with letters of marque. Again, the privateers captured more ships than the government; this time, however, the difference was eightfold rather than three.

The use of privateers sailing with letters of marque and reprisal was so important to the early American Republic that when the major European powers decided to ban privateering through the Treaty of Paris in 1856, the United States refused to sign on. The United States was concerned that without privateers, the government would have to raise and support an enormous standing navy. Not only would this be incredibly costly, but it also ran counter to the prevailing isolationist ideology of the time. As Yale law professor Nicholas Parrillo explains in an article about the history of privateering in the United States, Americans in the nineteenth century thought that a country with a standing army and navy would be more likely to find itself engaged in hostilities abroad. Many also felt that permanent military divisions would transfer money from the states to the federal government and from "virtuous farmers in the heartland" to "Eastern elites who financed the war debt and . . . giant industrial firms who sold warships, artillery, and other weapons." When Secretary of State William L. Marcy announced the nation's refusal to sign the Treaty of Paris, he declared that permanent navies, like permanent armies, were "detrimental to national prosperity and dangerous to civil liberty." Lots of people at the time even analogized private ships sailing under letters of marque to the iconic state and local militia. As Professor Parrillo intriguingly suggests, "[f]or many Americans, it seems, the clause of the Constitution authorizing 'letters of marque' had a purpose not unlike that of the Second Amendment, which guaranteed citizens the right to 'bear arms' in a 'militia' composed of laypersons organized in local communities, as opposed to professional warriors identified with the central state." Might it be more than just pure coincidence that Congressman Paul's call for revival of privateering in Somalia followed so closely on the heels of the Supreme Court's 2008 revitalization of the Second Amendment?

The United States didn't issue letters of marque and reprisal after the War of 1812, but until the late nineteenth century, the government still considered their use to be an active option in case of war. When it looked like the British might intervene in the Civil War on the side of the Confederacy, for example, the Union government threatened to use privateers against the interlopers, and Congress even passed a law authorizing President Lincoln to issue letters of marque, something he never ended up doing. The Confederacy, however, did issue letters of marque to private vessels, although the Union, viewing the conflict as an internal rebellion rather than a war between two sovereign states, refused to recognize these letters as legitimate. When the Union seized a ship called the *Savannah*, which was purportedly sailing under a letter of marque issued by the Confederacy, the Union government tried the captain and crew as pirates, much to the ire of the South. After the New York jury deadlocked, the Union decided not to retry the case, instead treating the captured crew as prisoners of war rather than pirates and ultimately exchanging them for Union prisoners of war held by the Confederacy. When the Civil War ended, the government promptly dismantled the large navy raised by the Union during the conflict, thus signaling that it still considered privateering to be preferable to raising a permanent navy. Some twenty-five years later, however, according to Professor Parrillo, the country's wariness about building a standing navy melted away. A major program of shipbuilding began around 1890, and the idea of using privateers ceased being a plausible alternative to official navy action . . . at least until Ron Paul revived the notion in 2008.

✺

The Egyptian plover is a small, cute, gray and orange bird that lives near rivers in sub-Saharan Africa and, according to *Wikipedia,* has a call that sounds like a "high-pitched *krrr-kirr-kirr.*" It's a nice bird, sure, but not a particularly unique or fascinating one when considered all by itself. What's most interesting about the Egyptian plover, however, is that apparently it shares a bizarre symbiotic relationship with the Nile crocodile. When the plover runs into a crocodile with its mouth open, the bird will hop inside and eat little pieces of meat out from between the reptile's teeth. The crocodile, which otherwise gets little in the way of dental hygiene, is happy to have the plover give it a teeth cleaning, and refrains from mashing the bird into a serving of delicious plover puree. Both animals reap a benefit—the plover gets an easy meaty meal, and the crocodile gets some much-needed oral sanitation work.

Like the Egyptian plover, the letters of marque and reprisal clause has been (until recently, anyway) interesting mainly because of its relationship with a far more prominent creature, in its case, the declare war clause, the constitutional equivalent of the Nile crocodile. Here's the full sentence containing both clauses: "*The Congress shall have Power . . . To declare War, grant Letters of Marque and Reprisal, and make Rules concerning Captures on Land and Water.*" As I talked about above, scholars have long debated whether the president can initiate armed hostilities with other nations without congressional authorization. It turns out that a lot of this debate has centered on the meaning of the letters of marque and reprisal clause, and specifically the relationship between that clause and its crocodilian neighbor.

Several prominent scholars have argued that the framers intended the letters of marque and reprisal clause to basically represent all forms of armed hostility short of full-out, congressionally declared war. On this theory, the framers put the two clauses right next to each other to show that all hostilities—whether they amount to actual war or instead something short of war—must be initiated by Congress and not the president. John Hart Ely might be the most prominent expert to make this type of argument. In his classic 1995 book *War and Responsibility: Constitutional Lessons of Vietnam and Its Aftermath,* Ely wrote that the "coupling of the war power with the power to grant letters of marque and reprisal underscores the founders' intention to require congressional authorization of military actions that fall short of what would conventionally have been counted wars." Notice how, to make this argument, it is necessary to construe the phrase "letters of marque and reprisal" very broadly, to cover not only authorizations from the government to private ships to fight pirates or the ships of other nations, but also any other type of armed conflict short of actual war. As another prominent writer puts it: "Letters of marque and reprisal were one way of referring to what were known as imperfect wars, special wars, limited wars—all of which constituted something less than full-scale warfare. . . . By including the Marque and Reprisal Clause in Article I, Section 8, the framers attempted to ensure that only Congress would have the power to commence armed hostilities against foreign nations."

Scholars on the other side of this question basically respond with something along the line of: *What? Are you kidding?* According to these critics, "letters of marque and reprisal" refer only to letters that authorize private ships to go fight other ships, not every possible kind of special, limited, imperfect war under the sun. If the authors of the Constitution had wanted it to say the latter, according to these writers, they would have been a lot clearer about it. As John Yoo reasonably argues (not everything he says is bewilderingly bananas): "Surely this goes too far. . . . Letters of marque and reprisal do not clearly refer to the use of the state's own military against another state. If the Framers had intended to place strict regulations on the public use of force in undeclared war situations, we can reasonably have expected them to use more direct, relevant language to express their meaning." Or, as a student at the University of Chicago Law School who then went on to be a deputy at OLC in the Bush administration explained, letters of marque were characterized by three features—an essentially commercial purpose (from the private ship's perspective), a lack of government funding, and legal control by prize courts—all of which are missing from the kinds of subwar "wars" that scholars like Ely have tried to fit under the letters of marque and reprisal clause.

I think the pro–executive branch "You school" has the better of this argument, but the pro-Congress school is more persuasive when it talks about the letters of marque and reprisal clause in relation to another constitutional crocodile— the commander in chief clause. Recall that the second main controversy when it comes to foreign affairs under the Constitution is whether the president has exclusive control over the prosecution of hostilities once they have begun. Here, the argument based on the letters of marque and reprisal clause goes something like this: At the time of the nation's founding, granting letters of marque and reprisal was an extremely important element of carrying out a war, as evidenced by the fact that many more ships during the Revolution were captured by American ships sailing with such letters than by ships sailing as part of the American Navy. If the pro-executive people are right about the framers wanting the president to have exclusive power to prosecute hostilities, then wouldn't we expect the framers to have given the letters of marque power to the president? Indeed, in England, the executive did have this power. But the framers instead chose to give the power to grant letters of marque and reprisal to Congress, thus signifying that they intended Congress to have at least some control over how the country carries out its wars. The commander in chief clause, then, does not give the president the exclusive power over the prosecution of hostilities.

A number of scholars have advanced this sort of argument. Jules Lobel of the University of Pittsburgh Law School, for example, has argued, "By providing Congress with the authority to issue such letters, the Framers gave Congress not only power over the initiation of warfare, but also over the conduct of naval warfare, in particular the power to determine who would be authorized to fight on behalf of the government, and the scope of and limitations of their authorization." Ingrid Brunk Wuerth of Vanderbilt concurs. She points out that the Articles of Confederation had authorized the executive (at that time, the states) to issue letters of marque during wartime but not during peace. The fact that the framers of the Constitution explicitly rejected this scheme and gave Congress the authority to issue letters during both peacetime and wartime, suggests that the framers were fine with creating "encroachments on the president's power to wage war." According to Wuerth, when they considered a foreign affairs power that would be potentially problematic under international law, the framers tended to give that power to Congress, rather than the president. Speaking of the letters of marque and reprisal clause (as well as the "captures clause," which is right next to it), Wuerth writes: "Contrary to many general formulations of the commander in chief power, the text of the Constitution did not leave to the president all decisions of tactics, military strategy, or deployment of force. Precisely where such decisions were most likely to violate international law and have significant diplomatic ramifications, the Constitution vested them in Congress."

Torture, by the way, is a violation of international law.

∽

So, what about Ron Paul's suggestion to revive letters of marque to fight pirates in Somalia? This wasn't actually the first time Paul has brought the idea up. Within a month of the 9/11 attacks, Paul proposed a bill that would have authorized letters of marque to be issued in response to "acts of air piracy." He proposed another similar bill in 2007; that legislation would have given the president the authority to grant letters of marque to "privately armed and equipped persons and entities . . . to employ all means reasonably necessary to seize outside the geographic boundaries of the United States and its territories the person and property of Osama bin Laden . . . and of any conspirator with Osama bin Laden and al Qaeda who are responsible for the air piratical aggressions and depredations perpetrated upon the United States of America on September 11, 2001." Like Paul's suggestion for dealing with Somali pirates, neither of these proposed bills having to do with "air piracy" made it very far in the legislative process.

Would granting letters of marque help the nation in its fight against sea piracy off the coast of Somalia? The answer turns on some very complicated concepts from the field of naval science. As experts in the field will tell you, the success of any given naval mission depends on the relationship of several key variables, including artillery power (A), flotilla size (S), mean rotation capacity of flotilla (R), and median nautical distance to relevant command centers (D). Scientists have expressed the overall "Command of the Sea" (C) metric in terms of these variables, as follows: $C = \Sigma \ (AS/DR_2)/\Omega$, where Ω stands for Ossinthrop's number, which every first-year naval strategy graduate student learns is 0.612387662.

Oh, wait a minute, what am I talking about? I don't know the first thing about naval science or strategy. I just made all that up.

In fact, I don't have any idea whether using privateers to fight pirates near Somalia would constitute sound naval policy. I mean, I would be worried about setting a bunch of gung-ho guys with maybe not all that much training in pirate fighting loose on the high seas with no supervision and a license to kill, particularly given our recent Blackwater-goes-haywire debacle in Iraq. I also agree with one critic of Paul's plan who wondered: "What happens when a ship flying under Congress accidentally takes out an aid ship bound for Somalia? At what time does an act seem pirate-like enough to cross the line? Do we really want these snap judgments being made on the fly in waters thousands of miles away from Washington? This is not Johnny Depp we're dealing with." But I am far from being an expert in this area. Who knows, maybe the government could solve these problems by providing adequate training and other safeguards. At least one military expert has suggested, in a sophisticated and balanced piece in an academic law journal, that with their "cost efficiency, flexibility, and technical skills," "[m]aritime security contractors can be part of the solution to piracy—especially if they are properly licensed and regulated through letters of marque."

What I do believe is that under the Constitution, issuing letters of marque and reprisal to fight piracy would be legally authorized. The situation is a little different now from the old days, because, as one commentator has put it, these days pirates "don't really have treasure chests, and their money is tied up in Swiss Bank accounts." To attract privateers, then, the government would have to offer up some significant reward money for captured pirates. There's also a question about whether Congress could delegate its power to grant letters of marque to the president, like Ron Paul has proposed. This might be one of those powers that has to stay with the branch provided for by the Constitution itself. And finally, there are international law issues to be concerned about, particularly given that most of the world voluntarily vowed over 150 years ago not to use privateers to fight pirates or anyone else. Still, though, the core idea that Congress could authorize private vessels to fight pirates on the government's behalf seems sound.

Imagine if scientists from an ornithology lab at the University of Texas published a paper concluding that we might be able to learn a lot about preventing human diabetes from studying the endocrine system of the Egyptian plover. All of a sudden, our interest in the plover would be transformed— no longer would we be interested in the bird just because of its relationship with the crocodile, but we would start studying the plover in its own right—for its own *ploverness,* its inherent *ploverocity.* In a way, Ron Paul's revival of the letters of marque and reprisal clause is sort of like this Egyptian plover scenario. Scholars have been interested in the clause for a long time because of what it might say about Congress and the president's respective powers under the declare war and commander in chief clauses. It remains interesting for that reason today. But Paul has suddenly made the clause interesting again in its own right. Could we really give letters of marque to private ships to fight pirates? Should we? What would these letters say, exactly? So far, Paul's proposals haven't gone anywhere, but under slightly different circumstances—more pirates, a navy engaged in war elsewhere, a different political climate—they might. As the letters of marque and reprisal clause story suggests, the line between constitutional songbird and constitutional crocodile may turn out to be an ephemeral one indeed.

CHAPTER 8

The Title of Nobility Clauses

Equality

No Title of Nobility shall be granted by the United States: And no Person Holding any Office . . . shall, without the consent of Congress, accept of any . . . Title, of any kind whatever, from any King, Prince, or foreign state.

Article I, Section 9

No State shall . . . grant any Title of Nobility.

Article I, Section 10

When Norman Schwarzkopf, commander of the allied forces in the first Gulf War, accepted an honorary knighthood from the queen of England in 1991, he may or may not have violated the Constitution. Most Americans, however, probably couldn't have cared less. After all, as a non-Brit, Schwarzkopf did not have to kneel before the queen or get his shoulder tapped with her royal sword. Foreigners who receive such an honor aren't even entitled to be called "dame" or "sir," although presumably plenty of people were used to calling Schwarzkopf "sir" already. In any event, Schwarzkopf was by no means the first US citizen to be knighted. Ronald Reagan, for instance, was knighted in 1989. Caspar Weinberger got his knighthood the year before. Eight military officers had received similar honors from the Crown prior to Schwarzkopf. And plenty of famous Americans from outside Washington have received knighthoods from all sorts of places over the years, from Jerry Lewis (France) to Mohammad Ali (Morocco) to Bob Hope (the Catholic Church). Still, though, there was something different about Schwarzkopf's knighthood. Unlike Bob Hope or Jerry Lewis, or even Reagan or Weinberger, who were retired when they received their honors, Schwarzkopf was still an officer of the United States in active service. Did his acceptance of the queen's honor therefore violate Article I, Section 9, of the Constitution? At least one skeptical journalist tried to find out, but he apparently didn't get very far. Christopher Hitchens, writing in the *Nation* shortly after Schwarzkopf's ceremony, explained that he had called the clerks of both houses of Congress, the Senate library, and various other officials to see if Congress had consented to Schwarzkopf's knighthood. Although someone eventually cited a congressional pronouncement that might be read to count as such consent, most people Hitchens talked to apparently had no idea such agreement was even required. "While it may not be possible to state with precision that General Schwarzkopf violated the Constitution by toadying to Queen Elizabeth," Hitchens concluded, "it is a sure thing that nobody in authority knows or cares whether he did or not."

One of the enduring themes of the modern US Constitution is that all people are created equal. Of course, this was not the case when the Constitution was first written. Slavery was not only accepted practice, but it was also explicitly recognized in the Constitution itself. It wasn't until 1865, in the aftermath of the Civil War, that the Thirteenth Amendment was added to the Constitution, thereby abolishing slavery throughout the nation. Beyond slavery, moreover, women were also not given full rights as citizens, and it wasn't until 1920 that the states ratified the Nineteenth Amendment, finally giving women the right to vote. The Thirteenth and Nineteenth amendments were hardly panaceas, however. Inequality, in all sorts of forms, continued to persist long after these legal changes, and real equality remains elusive even today.

The original Constitution does not contain any provision requiring that the government treat people equally. The equal-protection clause, which says that the government shall not "deny to any person . . . the equal protection of the laws," now plays that role, but it didn't become part of the Constitution until the states ratified the Fourteenth Amendment in 1868. That clause, of course, is one of the Constitution's superstars, a veritable giraffe among shrews, but it was not always so tall and spotted. For almost a hundred years, it slumbered silently in the Constitution like a tired shrew. Only in 1954, when the Court struck down segregated schools in *Brown v. Board of Education,* the most important decision of modern times, did the clause start living up to its potential. Since *Brown,* the Court has used the equal-protection clause to invalidate offensive laws like those prohibiting interracial marriage (*Loving v. Virginia*) and practices like striking potential jurors from the jury pool solely on account of their race (*Batson v. Kentucky*). More controversially, the Court has also used the equal-protection clause to strike down a variety of affirmative action programs intended to assist minorities, including race-based college-admission quotas and election districts drawn specifically to maximize the political representation of African Americans.

Starting in the 1970s, the Court also started using the equal-protection clause to scrutinize gender-based laws. This shift is attributable in large part to the pioneering work of Ruth Bader Ginsburg, who, as a practicing lawyer and the founder of the ACLU's Women's Rights Project, devised a successful strategy (often involving litigating cases on behalf of men, like the 3.2 percent beer case I described in chapter 6) to convince the Court to start treating gender-based laws much the same way it treats race-based laws. As a member of the Supreme Court, Justice Ginsburg cemented this approach to gender discrimination when she wrote the majority opinion in *United States v. Virginia*, which struck down Virginia Military Institute's male-only admissions policy. The Commonwealth of Virginia had argued that this policy was necessary to the continued viability of the school. Ginsburg disagreed, writing: "There is no reason to believe that the admission of women capable of all the activities required of VMI cadets would destroy the Institute rather than enhance its capacity to serve the 'more perfect Union.'"

Although the original Constitution fell far short of ensuring any sort of robust equality among citizens of the new republic, a few of its provisions at least aimed in that direction. The original text is at its most egalitarian when setting out qualifications for high public office. As we saw in chapter 5, just about anyone who can win an election can serve, regardless of background, religious conviction, or hereditary privilege. Another set of clauses that promote equality are the three (!) that cast aspersion on titles of nobility.

During the eighteenth century, the American colonists may have still enjoyed British tea, but they had little use for the complex hierarchical and hereditary social relationships of the English feudal system. A number of the nation's founders wrote eloquently on the subject. Thomas Paine, in his famous tract *Common Sense,* noted that monarchy was "the most preposterous invention the Devil ever set on foot for the promotion of idolatry," and that hereditary privileges were "an insult and an imposition on posterity." Alexander Hamilton, writing in *The Federalist Papers,* said that prohibiting American citizens from accepting titles of nobility was "the corner stone of republican government; for so long as they are excluded, there can never be serious danger that the government will be any other than that of the people." And James Madison said of the same prohibition that it was the "most decisive" proof of the republican nature of America's new democracy.

Congress had to face the "titles of nobility" issue head on almost immediately after independence. Trying to draft a response to George Washington's inaugural address, members of Congress had no idea what to call the country's new leader. They knew that "King Washington" was out, since Washington had previously rejected a suggestion that he refer to himself that way, but they argued vehemently about what they *should* call him. Some suggested "His Excellency," "His Highness, the President of the United States and Protector of their Liberties," or "His High Mightiness." These titles were all rejected. After much hand wringing, the Congress finally settled upon the nonnoble-and-boring-sounding "To the President of the United States."

The nation's earliest legal documents similarly demonstrate the colonists' opposition to titles of honor. Many colonies had adopted antinobility provisions in their own governing documents—the Massachusetts Constitution, for instance, observed that "the idea of a man born a magistrate, lawgiver, or judge, is absurd and unnatural"—and the Articles of Confederation contained one too. Unsurprisingly, the first draft of the new national Constitution included a flat-out ban on national titles of nobility. It read: "The United States shall not grant any title of nobility," and the final version, which reads much the same way, was approved with almost no discussion at all.

An early dispute involving a *private* hereditary organization shows just how much the early Americans detested titles of nobility. A couple of years after the end of the Revolution, a bunch of former officers of the Continental Army came together to form an organization called the Society of the Cincinnati (named after a famous Roman general), for the purpose of promoting the interests of former officers and providing general comradeship for those who had fought in the war. Only officers who had served for a certain amount of time were eligible to become members of the society, although under the organization's rules, the firstborn son of each member would also become part of the society. Members wore ribbons and medals, and between these sartorial flourishes, which were modeled on those worn by the French and British nobility, and the hereditary nature of the group, the Society of the Cincinnati looked to a lot of people like the creation of a new and dangerous noble class.

Accordingly, the country freaked out. John Adams said the society was "against the spirits of our governments and the genius of our people." Thomas Jefferson wrote a letter to George Washington in which he called the society contrary to "the natural equality of man." Benjamin Franklin said the former officers had created a hereditary knighthood that was "in direct Opposition to the solemnly declared Sense of their Country." Judges, governors, foreign ministers, historians, and newspaper writers joined in the attack against the society. An anti-society pamphlet written by the chief justice of South Carolina claimed that the society violated the title of nobility clause, even though it was a private organization, because it "usurp[ed] a nobility without gift or grant, in defiance of Congress and the States"; the pamphlet was widely distributed and, according to one commentator, was "enthusiastically embraced across the nation." When

George Washington, who was a member of the society, demanded during the group's first annual meeting in 1784 that the society abolish its hereditary provisions, the society bowed to pressure and briskly edited its founding document to do away with all mention of hereditary privilege.

Each of the three clauses relating to titles of nobility does something different. Article I, Section 10, prohibits the states from granting titles of nobility, and Article I, Section 9, prohibits the federal government from doing the same thing. The only restriction on receiving titles of nobility, as opposed to granting them, is the one contained at the end of Article I, Section 9, prohibiting officers of the United States from accepting titles of nobility granted by any king, prince, or foreign state without the consent of Congress. Interestingly, nothing in the Constitution prevents private individuals from receiving titles of nobility from foreign countries, which explains why Jerry Lewis could be made a commander in the French Legion of Honor (but doesn't explain why the French always found him so funny). Although private citizens don't violate the Constitution by accepting a foreign knighthood, it is worth nothing that US immigration law does require that any applicant for US citizenship who "has borne any hereditary title or has been of any of the orders of nobility in any foreign state" must renounce his or her title before becoming a citizen. Agency regulations even dictate the precise oath that such a foreign noble must utter. According to Title 8, Section 1337.1(d) of the Code of Federal Regulations, the applicant must say: "I further renounce the title of [give title or titles] which I have heretofore held" or (in the case of actual nobles), "I further renounce the order of nobility [give the order of nobility] to which I have heretofore belonged." As I am always telling my students, the Code of Federal Regulations, which contains all of the officially adopted regulations of the US government, is filled with this type of bizarre and fascinating stuff, like this definition of canned green beans from Volume 21, Section 955.120(a): "Canned green beans and canned wax beans are the foods prepared from the succulent pods of fresh green bean or wax bean plants conforming to the characteristics of phaseolus vulgaris L. and phaseolus coccineus L. The optimal color and varietal types and styles of the bean ingredient are set forth in paragraph (a)(2) of this section."

In law school, we professors like to use hypothetical examples to review the material we've just gone over. Oftentimes, the idea is to come up with the most ridiculous hypothetical imaginable, if for no other reason than to keep the class awake. In that spirit, consider the following. Back in 1972, a lieutenant in the elite Norwegian King's Guard, touring the Edinburgh Zoo in Scotland during an annual visit to a Scottish military music festival, picked out a particularly attractive and charismatic king penguin which he named Nils Olav and appointed as the Guard's official mascot in Edinburgh. Olav served as the honorary regimental sergeant major of the Guard from 1972 to 2005 and honorary colonel-in-chief from 2005 to mid-2008. In August of that year, the Guard decided a promotion was in order, and it conferred a knighthood upon the penguin (well, actually not the same exact penguin, but another penguin who had the same name and by all accounts looked kind of similar). Following a ceremony that featured speeches and apparently a review of the troops by the soon-to-be-anointed penguin, British Major General Euan Loudon, acting on behalf of Norway's King Harald V. Loudon, tapped the king's sword on both sides of the penguin's head, thus anointing the black-and-white waddler as an official, honest-to-goodness Knight of the Crown.

I am actually not that good at coming up with hypothetical examples, so I usually use a real-world problem instead, even if it's not exactly the best story to illustrate the legal point. And indeed this story about the penguin(s) is both true and also probably not the best story to illustrate the legal point. In any event, the question for our purposes is whether such a knighthood ceremony could happen in the United States. Although at first glance, the whole person-penguin distinction thing would seem to be an important issue, it really isn't. The title of nobility clauses directly restrict government entities; the clauses prohibit any government entity (whether federal or state) from granting a noble title. Apparently, then, a knighthood cannot be conferred by either the federal government or a state government, regardless of whether the intended conferee is a person, a potato, or a penguin. On the other hand, if it were the Norwegian government granting the knighthood, then anyone or anything could be the recipient, so long as the soon-to-be-knight were not already an officer of the United States (which presumably the penguin would not be). Of course, if Olav were ever to seek US citizenship, he would have to renounce his Norwegian title first. Anyway, the point is that only government officers are prohibited by the Constitution from holding titles of nobility from foreign countries. But what counts as an officer? We don't know exactly, because no court has ever been called upon to consider the issue. There are a couple of executive branch decisions, however, in which the attorney general or the OLC has opined on the question.

Back in 1911, for instance, a member of the House of Representatives named James McKinney wrote the secretary of state, asking whether a certain Professor J. A. Udden, the inventor of the Udden grade scale used to classify sedimentary rocks and at the time a special assistant to the US Geological Survey, could accept an offer from the king of Sweden to make him a "Knight of the North Star." The secretary forwarded McKinney's letter to Attorney General George W. Wickersham, who responded that because Udden's employment was intermittent and occasional rather than continuous, and because the geologist was paid by the day when actually employed ($5) rather than kept on salary, Udden was not an officer of the United States. "I have the honor," Wickersham wrote, "to advise you that there is nothing in the Constitution . . . to prevent the acceptance by Professor Udden of the order conferred upon him by the king of Sweden." Beyond this opinion, however, and a few others going back and forth on the question of whether members of advisory boards count as officers (right now the answer is that they don't), nobody has much considered the question of who precisely cannot accept a foreign title of nobility.

It is worth pausing here to remember that, according to the plain language of the Constitution, Congress can consent to an official accepting a title of nobility from abroad. In other words, if Congress agrees that some official can become a Knight of the Round Table or whatever, then the official is free to accept the honor. This is the theory that at least one government employee whom Christopher Hitchens spoke with about Norman Schwarzkopf relied on to defend the general's knighthood. The employee pointed Hitchens to (in Hitchens's words) "a surreptitious little piece of public law, enacted in 1966, that empowers bauble-hungry Americans to accept awards for soldiering 'subject to the approval of the department, agency, office or other entity in which such person is employed and the concurrence of the Secretary of State.'"

This quotation must refer to a somewhat antiquated version of the Foreign Gifts and Decorations Act, which expresses Congress's consent for certain government officials to accept a variety of foreign honors and gifts (Article I, Section 9, of the Constitution prohibits officials from accepting gifts as well as titles of nobility). The current version of the law (and the one in effect in 1991) says that an employee can accept, retain, and wear a "decoration tendered in recognition

of active field service in time of combat operations . . . subject
to the approval of the employing agency of such employee."
Did this statute bless Schwarzkopf's knighthood? Maybe,
maybe not. For one thing, it's not clear that the knighthood
conferred upon Schwarzkopf was only a "decoration." Even
if was just a decoration, moreover, it's also not clear whether
the Defense Department ever gave Schwarzkopf approval
to accept it. If not, then Schwarzkopf had violated the act,
possibly subjecting himself to a fine of up to $5,000, unless
Congress had consented to the knighthood in some other
way, something I have no intention of spending any of my
time trying to confirm or deny.

The limits placed on individuals by the title of nobility
clauses, then, turn out to be modest. Only officers of the
United States are prevented from accepting titles of nobility,
and then only if Congress doesn't consent. This limitation
was not nearly substantial enough for some of the early leaders of the Republic. The ratifying conventions of six states, in
fact, proposed amendments to the Constitution that would
have deleted the portion of Article I, Section 9, regarding
congressional consent. None of these proposed amendments
was adopted, but in 1810, two-thirds of both houses of Congress passed a proposed amendment that would have gone
even further than these early proposals. The so-called titles
of nobility amendment said this:

> If any citizen of the United States shall accept, claim,
> receive or retain any title of nobility or honour, or shall,
> without the consent of Congress, accept and retain
> any present, pension, office or emolument of any kind
> whatever, from any emperor, king, prince or foreign
> power, such person shall cease to be a citizen of the

United States, and shall be incapable of holding any office of trust or profit under them, or either of them.

If adopted, this language would have radically expanded the Constitution's prohibition on accepting titles of nobility. Not only would the proposal have eliminated the congressional-consent exception of the original Constitution (for titles of nobility at least, if not for presents and emoluments), but it would also have automatically deprived any recipient (not just officials) of US citizenship and prohibited the individual from becoming an officer of the federal government. Some have speculated that the impetus for the proposal was fear that the French government was going to confer a title upon the American wife of Napoleon Bonaparte's younger brother Jerome, but this theory does not seem to ever have been confirmed.

Fortunately for Norman Schwarzkopf and Jerry Lewis, the proposed thirteenth amendment was never ratified by enough states to become part of the actual Constitution. It came close, though, twice inching within two votes of being ratified by the required three-quarters of the states. In 1810 the Union had seventeen states; eleven of the required thirteen states ratified the amendment. New Hampshire ratified it in 1812, but by then Louisiana's entrance into the nation had raised the number of required ratifying states to fourteen. New Hampshire turned out to be the last state to ratify the proposed amendment, and by the time Rhode Island and South Carolina rejected the proposal in late 1814, it was clear that the titles of nobility amendment wasn't going anywhere.

This is not to say, however, that the amendment is even now completely dead. Consider the history of the Constitution's Twenty-seventh Amendment. This amendment—the most recent addition to the Constitution—was proposed by James Madison (yes, *that* James Madison) to limit the ability of members of Congress to grant themselves pay raises. The amendment, as passed by both houses of Congress and submitted to the states in 1789, stated that "No law varying the compensation for services of the Senators and Representatives, shall take effect, until an election of the Representatives shall have intervened." A few states ratified the amendment, but not nearly enough for it to become law, and after about 1792, the amendment laid mostly dormant until it was rediscovered by a student at the University of Texas in the early 1980s (yes, *those* 1980s). A movement developed to get the amendment ratified, and over the next decade or so, over thirty states approved it, with Alabama putting the amendment over the top on May 5, 1992, a mere 203 years after the language was submitted to the states.

If the Twenty-seventh Amendment can become law hundreds of years after it was submitted to the states, presumably the original thirteenth amendment could enjoy the same fate. After all, the titles of nobility amendment—like the Twenty-seventh Amendment, but unlike the doomed equal rights amendment of the early 1970s—was unaccompanied by any explicit congressional deadline for its ratification. If you truly hate the idea of American citizens receiving foreign honorary titles, and if you happen to have a whole lot of extra time on your hands, you might consider spearheading a movement to get the forgotten titles of nobility amendment back on the nation's front burner.

Although the titles of nobility amendment was never ratified by a sufficient number of states and therefore never became part of the Constitution, it came close enough to cause some serious confusion over the two hundred years since its proposal. In 1815 the editor of the new version of the *United States Statutes at Large*, which is the official collection of the nation's laws, was unable to figure out if the amendment had in fact been ratified. Noting that the information provided to him by the government was "defective" to show "whether the amendment proposed . . . has, or has not, been adopted by a sufficient number of the state legislatures to authorize its insertion as part of the constitution," editor John Colvin decided to publish the amendment as though it had been ratified, although he accompanied the printed amendment with an explanation that he just wasn't sure about its status.

Recently, certain people who seem to dislike lawyers even more than most people dislike lawyers have started latching onto the titles of nobility amendment in a frivolous but sort of frightening way. These individuals have tried to argue, in print and even before courts, that the term "esquire" as it is used by lawyers is in fact a title of nobility and that all lawyers have therefore been deprived of their citizenship by the titles of nobility amendment, the actual ratification of which has been purposely covered up by, well, lawyers. One of the leading proponents of this view is a guy who, according to one account, will demand full-blown trials on behalf of defendants accused of things like speeding or illegal fishing, and then put forward as a defense the unconstitutionality of the entire legal system. Luckily, claims like these haven't worked so well, since it's absolutely clear both that "esquire" is not a title of nobility and that the titles of nobility amendment was never ratified. As one judge put it in response to a defendant's claim that neither the judge nor the prosecutor (nor even members of Congress, for that matter) were US citizens authorized to administer anything having anything to do with the American legal system, "these arguments may be amusing to some but are meritless and must be rejected."

The "esquire" argument may be frivolous, but it does raise an interesting and important question, which is, What actually counts as a title of nobility, anyway? What exactly are states and the federal government prohibited from granting? It's clear that the government can't make someone a king or a duke or an earl, but is there anything short of these classic titles that should be considered a "title of nobility" for constitutional purposes? Are there practices out there, real or potential, that might violate the same equality principles that animated the framers to enact the constitutional ban on titles of nobility, and if so, what are they?

You might think that the courts would have addressed this issue, but they haven't. The judicial opinions that exist mostly consist of not much more than cursory rejections of clearly frivolous arguments. One court, for instance, rejected out of hand a defendant's contention that the military rank system was a title of nobility (he had been convicted for refusing to report for duty). Another dismissed without much discussion the argument that the title of "magistrate" was a noble one. And the Supreme Court of Nebraska in 1988 got so sick of hearing title of nobility claims from people convicted of driving without a license that it dedicated an entire paragraph to explaining why driver's licenses are not titles of nobility. "A driver's license has no connection with social rank," the court explained, and "bestows nothing more than the authority to operate a motor vehicle."

Perhaps the only recorded judicial decision in the history of the Republic to rely on the title of nobility clauses in any way to forbid someone from doing something is a case called *In re Jama*, which is also one of the strangest opinions I've ever read in my life. A guy named Robert Paul Jama, who alleged that "somewhere, sometime, in the past his deceased father told him that the family name was originally von Jama but that the von part had been dropped," applied back in 1966 to a civil court in New York to change his name to Robert von Jama. He wanted to "Germanize his patronymic" (all the quotes here are directly from the opinion) because he wanted a "German genealogy" and because "his friends and acquaintances [were] all of Germanic stock." The judge rejected Jama's application, relying on a combination of anti-

Germanic prejudice and jingoism, with a splash of the title of nobility clauses thrown in for good measure. I can't help myself from quoting the bizarre opinion at length:

> The moral guilt of the Germanic peoples in adopting the philosophies of a monstrosity and his cohorts has not yet been fully eradicated or been forgotten ... The court does not intend by these observations to condemn an entire nation nor its people but cannot reconcile petitioner's desire to affiliate himself with such close affinity with the von. . . . If a man is going to be an American at all, he should be so without any qualifying adjectives. . . . An American should measure himself by the American standard, and paraphrasing the bold Romans of old, proudly proclaim himself Civis Americanus Sum. . . . Article I, section 9, clause 8, United States Constitution prohibits the grant of any title of nobility by the United States. . . . It would be presumptuous if not unlawful for this court to take a position or do an act contrary to the spirit and intent, if not the letter, of our Federal Constitution. . . . Reflection should indicate to the applicant that his reasons for a change are puerile, if not pathetic.

All this silly stuff about the driver's licenses and the "von" and so on are ridiculous, but some serious questions do exist about what kinds of things beyond the obvious titles like duke or earl are prohibited by the clauses. Legal scholars over the years have proposed some possibilities for what kinds of practices—both current and future hypothetical—might be prohibited by the Constitution's prohibition on official noble titles.

For instance, what about the practice, engaged in by probably every state university in the country, of granting legacy preferences to children and grandchildren of alumni?

According to one source, top universities have a double, triple, or even quadruple acceptance rate for legacies than for ordinary applicants. It's no secret why universities do this—it's a great way to encourage alumni to contribute money and, in some cases, libraries, science centers, or stadiums. But it surely doesn't seem fair to those of us whose parents didn't happen to go to the school we would like to attend. Why should the son or granddaughter of a University of Virginia graduate have a better chance of admission than anyone else? The practice is particularly troublesome since it benefits white students to the detriment of minorities, whose parents and grandparents are far less likely to have attended a top school than William "Skip" Preston Westinghouse III. Although legacy preferences harm minorities, they cannot be reached by the equal-protection clause, because the Court has interpreted that provision to prohibit only intentional discrimination, rather than practices that merely have the *effect* of harming minorities.

Recently, however, a scholar at the University of California at Davis, Carlton F. W. Larson, has argued that the title of nobility clauses should prohibit state universities from granting legacy preferences. Conceding the novelty of his suggestion—Larson writes early on in his article: "Titles of nobility? Surely only cranks and misfits invoke the Nobility Clauses in constitutional argument"—Larson argues that the nobility clauses should be read broadly to prohibit "hereditary privileges with respect to the institutions of the state," and that legacy preferences "fail miserably" under this restriction. Larson's article was so intriguing that it had the rare distinction of being picked up by the nation's most important newspaper. Writing in the *New York Times*, Adam Liptak called Larson's argument "fascinating and provocative," although he ultimately seemed dubious. "It still seems a bit of a leap," Liptak wrote, "to move from prohibiting the government from naming me a duke to barring public universities from giving the children of alumni an admissions advantage."

Here's another possibility. What if the government decided to create a class of biologically superior citizens by funding and then selectively distributing certain types of genetic services (cloning, organ transplants, "Nobel Prize Sperm Banks," and who knows what other sci-fi possibilities there might be) to those who could afford to pay enormous sums? Would this have the effect of producing a "noble" class of citizens that would be able to pass down their advantages from generation to generation? Should the title of nobility clauses have anything to say about this?

Richard Delgado, one of the nation's most prominent and creative legal scholars, considered this question back in the mid-1980s, and argued that courts might use the clauses to stop such practices. According to Delgado, distribution of certain biological benefits by the government to wealthy individuals might create "a rapid, drastic, and probably irreversible widening of the gap between society's haves and have nots," since "[t]he beneficiaries would receive a substantial and much-desired benefit, the effects may be long-lasting, and the recipients could come to be viewed as naturally and deservedly superior." The equal-protection clause might not be sufficient to stop the practice, because at least thus far, the government is allowed to distinguish among people on the basis of their wealth. Perhaps the title of nobility clauses, following in the footsteps of the equal protection clause's sudden emergence from nowhere in 1954, would have to step up, grow a neck, become a giraffe, and save us from ourselves. Wouldn't it be something if one of our Constitution's odd clauses was the only obstacle standing in the way of an American *Brave New World*?

CHAPTER 9

The Bill of Attainder Clauses

Liberty

No Bill of Attainder ... shall be passed [by Congress].

Article I, Section 9

No State shall ... pass any Bill of Attainder.

Article I, Section 10

Consider the following three stories from recent years:

After the Supreme Court held in 2006 that the Bush administration could not try "enemy combatants" in military tribunals created solely through executive order, Congress passed a statute establishing "military commissions" and providing that the president could try "alien unlawful enemy combatants" in front of them. Under the statute, these commissions have some of the procedural protections of so-called "real" courts, but not all of them. For instance, while the defendant, unlike with Bush's tribunals, does have the right to attend commission proceedings, the government may introduce "evidence" (here, imagine that I'm making grotesquely exaggerated quote marks with my fingers) like hearsay and statements obtained from the defendant by coercion—that judges generally do not allow in real courts. Guantanamo detainees like Salim Ahmed Hamdan (Bin Laden's personal driver) and Khalid Sheikh Mohammed brought all sorts of constitutional challenges to the statute in front of both the commissions themselves and real courts. Among other things, these detainee-defendants argued that Congress, by naming a class of people (alien unlawful enemy combatants) and authorizing them to be tried in front of commissions with limited procedural protections, had violated the Constitution's ban on bills of attainder ("attainder" is an old English word meaning "taintedness").

In 2009, following a year in which the insurance giant AIG posted the all-time biggest loss in corporate history and then received $182 billion in government bailout money, the company announced that it was awarding nearly $200 million in bonuses to its traders so they could buy fancy cheese and Jaguars. The country went ballistic. President Obama called the move an "outrage." Republican senator Chuck Grassley urged the company's officers to do as the Japanese do in such situations—bow and apologize, and then maybe commit suicide. Shortly after the company's announcement, the House of Representatives, by a wide margin, passed a law that would have imposed a 90 percent tax on most bonuses issued by companies, like AIG, that had received over $5 billion in government bailouts. Critics of the proposal cited a variety of policy and constitutional objections to the tax. Among other things, these commentators argued that Congress, by authorizing a gigantic tax on a specific group of people, had violated the Constitution's ban on bills of attainder.

In the closing years of the last century, executives at the Association of Community Organizations for Reform Now, better known as ACORN, covered up the fact that the brother of the group's founder had embezzled almost a million dollars from the organization. When this became public knowledge in 2008, it was only the beginning of ACORN's troubles. Allegations surfaced that ACORN, which received about 10 percent of its operating funds from the federal government, had engaged in voter fraud, tax law violations, and other dastardly activities. The group hit rock bottom in 2009, when hidden-camera videos showed ACORN employees in Baltimore supposedly explaining to a prostitute and her pimp how they could set up their business to evade IRS scrutiny. Not cool. Congress responded to ACORN's difficulties by providing that no federal agency could give any money to "ACORN, or any of its affiliates, subsidiaries, or allied organizations." ACORN then sued the government, claiming that by singling out the organization for special negative treatment under its appropriation laws, Congress had violated the Constitution's ban on bills of attainder.

According to the Supreme Court, "legislative acts, no matter what their form, that apply either to named individuals or to easily ascertainable members of a group in such a way as to inflict punishment on them without a judicial trial are bills of attainder prohibited by the Constitution." In which of the three just-described scenarios, if any, did Congress enact a forbidden bill of attainder?

The Constitution, as it reads today, is downright lousy with protections for individual liberty. You can hardly swing a cat around the document without hitting one. The Constitution protects our freedom to speak freely, to practice the religion of our choice, and to associate with whomever we want. It keeps the police from searching us unreasonably and requires the government to provide all sorts of procedural protections—the right to a lawyer, for instance, and to confront hostile witnesses—before it can convict us of a crime. It says that before the state takes away our property or liberty, we must be given notice and some kind of a hearing, aka "due process of law." Hell, the Constitution might even protect our God-given right to fire off a few rounds of an automatic machine-gun.

If you look closely, however, you will see that almost all of these procedural protections are located in the Bill of Rights—the first ten amendments to the Constitution, added as a group in 1791. The original Constitution contains very few provisions that explicitly protect individual freedoms. Many federalists, the Constitution's original supporters, saw no need for such provisions, figuring that the document's many structural provisions (separating the branches, separating federal power from state power) were already adequate to protect individual liberties. The federalists also apparently thought that the Constitution's limited grant of power to the federal government made it unlikely that individual freedoms would be in danger. After all, these supporters argued, nothing in the Constitution affirmatively gives Congress or the president the power to infringe anyone's liberty, so what's to worry? Fortunately, when it became clear that the Constitution's early success was going to turn on the support of a sufficient number of anti-federalists, most of whom supported a bill of rights, the skeptical framers gave in and agreed to put together a nice little package of individual liberties to tack on to the original document.

The original Constitution does, however, contain a couple of important, if quirky, liberty-protecting clauses. There are the "ex post facto clauses" of Article I, for example, which make it unconstitutional for either the federal or state governments to inflict retroactive punishment. In other words, if you do something today that's not currently illegal—say, texting while riding a motorcycle—the government cannot pass a law tomorrow outlawing motorcycle texting and then punish you for having broken it yesterday. You need to be on notice that you can be punished for something before the government can punish you for it. That's a handy protection to have in the Constitution, and it says something about the propensity of eighteenth-century legislatures to inflict retroactive punishment that the framers singled it out as one of the very few liberty-depriving practices that they forbade in the original Constitution.

Of course, as with all constitutional clauses (remember the discussion of the seemingly simple "you have to be thirty-five years old to be president" clause from chapter 5), the ex post facto clauses raise some difficult interpretive questions. For example, what exactly counts as "punishment"? Putting someone in prison to exact retribution for a terrible crime is clearly punishment, but what about putting someone deemed irrevocably dangerous into some kind of civil confinement situation after they are released from prison as a way of protecting potential victims? Many states have laws that do this sort of thing to sex offenders, and even though those laws were passed, in some cases, after the offenders had been convicted for their sex offenses, the Supreme Court has held that they do not inflict punishment in violation of the ex post facto clauses. I happen to think that's crazy, and not just because this was the position I was assigned to take in my law school moot court competition fifteen years ago, a tournament that stressed me out so much I had to gulp down a shot of vodka before a particularly nerve-wracking round, but that's the Supreme Court for you. (I'll spare you the story of how one judge during the competition, on a 1–10 scale, gave me a 5 for "appearance.")

As we will see, this "what is punishment" issue also becomes very important when dealing with the bill of attainder clauses, which are found, not surprisingly, right next to the ex post facto clauses, as in Article I, Section 9: *No Bill of Attainder or ex post facto Law shall be passed.*

In sixteenth- through eighteenth-century England, a bill of attainder was a legislative enactment sentencing an individual or a group of individuals to death for committing treason without any kind of judicial trial whatsoever. If you can believe it, receiving one of these bills was even worse than it might sound at first. For one thing, bills of attainder came accompanied by something called a "corruption of blood," which meant that the state, rather than the individual's heirs, would receive the accused's property after death. Moreover, the death sentence itself tended toward the brutal. No purportedly painless and medicalized lethal-injection procedure for the recipient of a bill of attainder in old England. An apparently typical punishment for men convicted of treason in the eighteenth century:

> You are to be drawn upon a hurdle to the place of execution, and there you are to be hanged by the neck, and being alive cut down, and your privy-members to be cut off, and your bowels to be taken out of your belly and there burned, you being alive; and your head to be cut off, and your body to be divided into four quarters, and that your head and quarters be disposed of where his majesty shall think fit.

For God's sake, not the privy-members. Hands off the privy-members! Incidentally, women convicted of treason were merely "burned with fire until . . . dead." Anyway, in addition to the bill of attainder, English practice also allowed Parliament to enact a law punishing someone with something a bit lighter than death by disembowelment and decapitation. This kind of law, known as a "bill of pains and penalties," might have sentenced the unfortunate recipient to some time in prison or banished the person from civil society or even just taken away his or her right to vote. As with bills of attainder, the targeted individual was not entitled to a day in court or any other procedural protections before the punishment was inflicted.

You might think the American colonies, having revolted against the tyranny of the British, would have immediately done away with legislative punishment, but this was not the case. Indeed, experts claim that bills of attainder were even more popular here around the time of the Revolution than they ever were in England. In 1776 Pennsylvania passed almost five hundred bills of attainder against Tories accused of treason. New York passed a law in 1779 sentencing more than fifty people to death, including two former governors, for having supported King George III, "with Intent to subvert the Government and Liberties of this State."

The most interesting bill of attainder ever passed by an American colony or state was one from Virginia that was pushed through the legislature by none other than Mister Freedom himself, Thomas Jefferson. In the summer of 1777, an English sympathizer named Josiah Philips and a team of bandits were wreaking terror on the populations of Princess Anne and Norfolk counties in southeastern Virginia. According to one Virginia lawyer, writing in 1910, Philips

> carried on a species of warfare against the innocent and defenseless, at the bare mention of which humanity shudders. Scarcely a night passed without witnessing the shrieks of women and children, flying by the light of their own burning houses, from the assaults of these merciless wretches; and every day was marked by the desolation of some farm, by robberies on the highway, or the assassination of some individual whose patriotism had incurred the displeasure of this fierce and bloody leader of outlaws.

Unfortunately for the innocent and defenseless, the government had no success in capturing Philips and his gang.

The group took cover in a place called Dismal Swamp (now the Great Dismal Swamp National Wildlife Refuge) that was just too difficult for the government to penetrate, and there were also lots of Tories in the area who were willing to hide the bad guys. In May of 1778, Patrick Henry, Virginia's governor, asked the state legislature to pass a bill of attainder against Philips to aid with his capture and punishment. The bill that ended up passing the legislature was written by Jefferson, who at the time was a legislative delegate from Albemarle County. The law gave Philips until July 1 to report to the authorities or else be "convicted and attained of high treason, and shall suffer the pains of death." Not only that, but Jefferson decided to basically deputize the entire population as officers of the state, making it legal for anyone who came across Philips to kill him and his buddies on the spot: "*Be it further enacted,* That from and after the passage of this act, it shall be lawful for any person, with or without orders to pursue and slay the said Josiah Philips, and any others who have been of his associates or confederates."

As it turned out, Philips was captured in the fall, but Attorney General Edmund Randolph decided to forgo the attainder law and try him in a court of law. Randolph didn't think he had the evidence to convict Philips of murder or arson, so he opted instead to try him and his gang of stealing (the evidence showed that they had taken twenty-eight hats and five pounds of twine). The jury found Philips guilty, and since even hat and twine robbery was punishable by death (sounds like modern-day Texas), he and his fellow ruffians were hanged before the end of the year. Although the attainder law was never used, Jefferson continued to justify his decision to support the bill throughout his life, writing at one point many years after the incident that he "was then thoroughly persuaded of the correctness of this proceeding, and am more and more convinced by reflection."

c∕∕∕o

Despite Jefferson's flirtation with legislative punishment, it is easy to see why the framers would have had it in for bills of attainder, because these things fed right into their loathing of concentrated powers. Unlike the framers' ideal vision of how the government should mete out punishment—the legislature makes a general rule, the executive charges someone with violating the rule, and the courts decide if the rule has really been broken—with bills of attainder, the legislature acts completely alone. Moreover, because legislatures are elected by popular vote and lack the kinds of procedural protections found in courts, the framers thought that they were inherently inadequate to determine individual guilt. No wonder James Madison called bills of attainder "contrary to the first principles of the social compact" and Alexander Hamilton said that to apply the "name of liberty" to any government that used them "would be a mockery of common sense."

At the outset, though, it was far from clear whether, by using the specific phrase "bills of attainder" in the Constitution, rather than something broader, like "legislative punishment," the framers had outlawed only those legislative enactments that precisely resembled the English bills of attainder. Would a legislative death sentence that didn't carry with it a "corruption of blood" count? (Interestingly, a separate section of Article III provides that "Congress shall have Power to declare the Punishment of Treason, but no Attainder of Treason shall work Corruption of Blood.") How about a legislatively imposed prison sentence or property forfeiture? The Supreme Court answered this question definitively very early on, when Chief Justice Marshall, in the 1810 decision of *Fletcher v. Peck,* stated that a "bill of attainder may affect the life of an individual, or may confiscate his property, or may do both." The Court made it clear that the clause was aimed at the problem of legislative punishment generally and not just the specific bad thing known as a "bill of attainder" in eighteenth-century England.

The Court has heard a number of bill-of-attainder-clause cases in the last couple of hundred years, but only five times has it ever condemned a law under the provision. The first two of these cases came right after the Civil War. In *Cummings v. Missouri,* the Court struck down a law making it illegal for anyone who could not swear an oath that he had not rebelled against the Union to serve in certain professions, including the priesthood. In *Ex parte Garland,* the Court invalidated a federal statute that required any lawyer who wanted to appear in federal court to take the same kind of oath. Building on *Fletcher v. Peck,* the Court in these two decisions made clear that the bill of attainder clauses would be applied broadly, not only to a punishment that is far, far less severe than the death penalty, but also to laws that describe a group of people rather than naming them specifically. Another famous bill of attainder case came in 1946, in *United States v. Lovett,* when the Court struck down a law that singled out three specific government officers, deemed by at least one member of Congress to be "irresponsible, unrepresentative, crackpot, radical bureaucrats" (read: Communists) as being unfit, and therefore ineligible, for a federal salary. "Those who wrote our Constitution," the Court said in striking down the law, "well knew the danger inherent in special legislative acts which take away the life, liberty, or property of particular named persons, because the legislature thinks them guilty of conduct which deserves punishment."

The high point for the bill of attainder clauses came in 1965, when the Court held that Congress could not make it a crime for a member of the Communist Party to hold an officer or employee position in a labor union. The case involved a San Francisco dockworker named Archie Brown, who had been a Communist since the late 1920s. When Brown was elected to the executive board of his union, he was charged with violating a 1959 labor statute and sentenced to six months in prison. Brown, who had fought as a machine gunner in the Spanish Civil War and at the Battle of the Bulge during World War II, not surprisingly refused to back down and challenged his conviction on constitutional grounds. In a landmark opinion, Chief Justice Earl Warren rejected the government's position that because the law was intended not as retribution but rather as a way of keeping dangerous people out of positions where they could do harm, it did not impose "punishment." As Warren wrote, "Punishment serves several purposes; retributive, rehabilitative, deterrent—and preventive. One of the reasons society imprisons those convicted of crimes is to keep them from inflicting future harm, but that does not make imprisonment any the less punishment."

In several other cases, however, the Supreme Court has rejected bill of attainder challenges to controversial laws. In a 1984 case called *Selective Service System v. Minnesota PIRG*, for instance, the Court upheld a federal law that made male students who hadn't registered for the draft ineligible for student financial aid. Why was this different from the laws struck down in previous cases? The Court cited two reasons. First, unlike *Cummings* or *Garland*, where someone had either fought for the Confederacy or not, here someone who wanted federal aid could change his mind and register for the draft. Thus, the group of people singled out under the law was not permanently set at the time of the legislation. Second, the law did not impose punishment, primarily because it served the nonpunitive goal of encouraging young men to register for the draft. In deciding that the law was not punishment, the Court applied a three-part test (the Supreme Court loves three-part tests almost as much as it loves big corporations) that was set out several years before in *Nixon*

v. Administrator of General Services, a case in which Richard
Nixon unsuccessfully challenged a law singling out his papers and tapes for special treatment. According to the test
set out in *Nixon* and applied in *Selective Service System,* the
question of whether some burden imposed by a law counts
as "punishment" turns on whether (1) the burden has *historically* been considered punishment; (2) the burden *functions*
as punishment (or whether it instead serves some nonpunitive goal); and (3) the legislature *intended* to punish the
individual or individuals singled out by the law. These, then,
are the key questions when it comes to deciding whether
the three scenarios described at the beginning of the chapter
were constitutional.

Assuming that you are alive and have not been sleeping under a rock for the past twenty years, you know that the statute books in this country are filled with laws that single out
gays and lesbians for negative treatment, denying them the
right to marry and many other benefits enjoyed by opposite-
sex couples. Might these laws be subject to attack under the
bill of attainder clauses?

In 1992, residents of Colorado passed a referendum
amending the state's constitution to provide that no government unit within the state "shall enact, adopt or enforce any
statute, regulation, ordinance or policy whereby homosexual,
lesbian or bisexual orientation, conduct, practices or relationships shall . . . entitle any person or class of persons to have or
claim any minority status, quota preferences, protected status
or claim of discrimination." The referendum, called Amendment 2, rendered invalid local ordinances in Aspen, Boulder,
and Denver that had outlawed discrimination on the basis of
sexual orientation in areas like employment, public accom-
modation, and education.

Opponents of the new law (here, we will refer to them as "people who believe in goodness rather than badness") challenged it in federal court, arguing that it violated the equal protection clause of the Fourteenth Amendment. Despite the inherent goodness of these challengers, they had an uphill road to travel to get the law invalidated under that clause, because the Court had never previously frowned upon laws discriminating against gays and lesbians. Indeed, in 1986, in a debacle of a decision called *Bowers v. Hardwick,* the Court had upheld against constitutional attack Georgia's conviction of a man under the state's sodomy law for engaging in anal and/or oral sex with another man in his own bedroom. (This decision, mercifully, was overruled in 2003.)

The Supreme Court surprised a lot of people when it decided in *Romer v. Evans* that Amendment 2 did in fact violate the equal protection clause. Justice Kennedy's opinion for the majority, however, did not fashion any sort of broad ruling to protect gays and lesbians from run-of-the-mill discrimination. Instead, the Court focused on the specifically awful nature of Amendment 2—a law so broad and so unconnected to any plausible justification that it "seems inexplicable by anything but animus toward the class it affects." The Court, essentially, invented a new doctrine to deal with Amendment 2—the "anti-animus" rule—that it had never used before and has not used since. It probably goes without saying that Justice Scalia issued a dissenting opinion so apoplectic in tone that one wonders whether he bit a gavel in half while writing it.

Because the majority's decision in *Romer* strayed pretty far from traditional equal protection doctrine, even scholars who supported the decision looked for ways to explain it that might make better sense of the case. One such scholar was Yale Law's Akhil Amar, a constitutional law professor so prominent that I'm surprised I haven't mentioned him yet. If Amar were a baseball player, he'd be Alex Rodriguez; if he were a Scrabble player, he'd be, well, whoever one of the best Scrabble players in the country is. In an article published soon after *Romer* was decided, called "Attainder and Amendment 2: *Romer's* Rightness," Amar argued that the key to understanding the case is the Constitution's ban on bills of attainder, which is essentially what Amendment 2 amounted to. Amar wrote of the law: "It was a kind of legal and social outlawry in cowboy country—a targeting of outsiders, a badge of second-class citizenship, a tainting of queers, a scarlet Q. The queer (pun intended) language of Amendment 2—its odd and obsessive singling out of all nonstandard sexual orientations—was a subtle cue, a Freudian slip that told fashioned animus was afoot here." Though Amar observed that Justice Kennedy's opinion didn't actually discuss or even mention the bill of attainder clause, he argued that "the sociology and principles underlying the Attainder Clause powerfully illuminate . . . the opinions in *Romer,* and the spirit of the Equal Protection itself." The clause, Amar suggested, "offers lawyers litigating gay rights cases a particularly rich and apt source of doctrine."

Amar's article got a lot of attention in the lawyerly and scholarly world, and, sure enough, lawyers litigating gay rights cases have tried using his attainder theory to challenge other anti-gay-and-lesbian laws and regulations. Once, it almost even worked. In the year 2000, the charitable citizens of Nebraska (probably the same people who keep arguing that a driver's license is a title of nobility) voted by a huge majority to amend their constitution to make sure that people of the same sex who love each other cannot enjoy the same legal benefits enjoyed by people of different sexes who love each other. Specifically, the new Section 29 of the Nebraska state constitution says that: "Only marriage between a man and a woman shall be valid or recognized in Nebraska. The uniting of two persons of the same sex in a civil union, domestic partnership, or other similar same-sex relationship shall not be valid or recognized in Nebraska."

As in Colorado, people who believe in goodness sued, and at first the courts agreed that the new law violated the US Constitution. District court judge Joseph Bataillon held that Section 29 violated the First Amendment, the Fourteenth Amendment, and the bill of attainder clause. On the latter holding, he agreed with the plaintiffs that by making it impossible for them to "petition their representatives and city and local governments for legislative changes that would protect their relationships, agreements, and interests," the new amendment "effectively disenfranchised lesbian and gay and bisexual people and their supporters." Citing the Supreme Court's decision in *Brown* and prominently featuring Amar's article on *Romer,* Judge Bataillon concluded that this was punishment aimed at a specific group. The Eighth Circuit Court of Appeals, however, disagreed and found fault with almost everything that the district court had said. On the bill of attainder point, the appeals court held that the political disadvantage imposed on gays and lesbians by Section 29 was punishment neither in the historical sense nor in the functional sense. Why didn't the amendment serve functionally to punish? Because "it serves the nonpunitive purpose of steering heterosexual procreation into marriage, a purpose that negates any suspicion that the supporters of [the amendment] were motivated solely by a desire to punish disadvantaged groups."

I'm not sure what I think about this bill of attainder argument against laws disadvantaging gays and lesbians. I find myself agreeing with New York University's Rick Hills, who filed a brief on behalf of the plaintiffs in *Romer* arguing that Amendment 2 violated the equal protection clause. In an article responding to Amar's bill of attainder clause analysis, Hills (a former student of Amar's) suggests, among other things, that the Coloradoans who supported and voted for Amendment 2 did not think that they were targeting a closed class of individuals; indeed, one reason they disliked giving rights to gays and lesbians was because they feared these rights would cause more people to "become gay." Regardless of the nutso-ness of this fear, it does suggest that the supporters of the amendment did not seek to punish a specific, closed set of people through their nasty law, which is the essence of a bill of attainder. More to the point, though, I feel that a judicial decision using the bill of attainder clause to strike down a law like Colorado's or Nebraska's would skirt the real issue, which is that gays and lesbians deserve equal treatment under the law. Much better, I think, for the courts to strike down obnoxious laws like Amendment 2 on straightforward equal protection clause grounds. Sometimes a problem as gross as outright discrimination on the basis of sexual orientation deserves to be fed to the constitutional lions.

So, what about the three scenarios from the beginning of the chapter? The Military Commissions Act is probably not a bill of attainder. The argument of many Guantanamo detainees was that the statute punished them by singling them out as a class for a trial without the full range of procedural rights given to most accused criminals. As Khalid Sheikh Mohammed argued in 2008 before a military judge, for instance, "Congress's creation of a trial system, long after the alleged conduct of these Accused, employing specially-tailored rules of evidence and procedure designed to ensure their conviction, is plainly 'punishment,' imposed upon the Accused by legislative enactment without judicial trial." The argument is mildly plausible, but no judge has ever accepted it, and it is unlikely ever to succeed. For one thing, the military has always had a justice system where defendants are given fewer rights than defendants receive in civilian courts. If singling out Guantanamo detainees for trials with fewer rights is a bill of attainder, then wouldn't the same thing be true for singling out military personnel for such trials? The Supreme Court has never suggested that the current military system of justice is unconstitutional. And while I'm not a big supporter of giving criminal defendants fewer rights during trial, I don't think that taking away a right here or there is itself something that has historically or otherwise been considered "punishment." Thus, I'm not at all surprised that the military judges who ruled on the constitutionality of the Military Commissions Act rejected the bill of attainder argument out of hand. President Obama has announced his intention to try the Guantanamo detainees before real courts rather than the military commissions. Thus, the detainees will likely no longer have any basis to raise the argument, unless Congress forces the president to try them at Gitmo.

The AIG tax-the-bonuses-at-a-gazillion-percent thing is a closer case, and again we will never know what the courts would have said (no such bill was ever enacted into law), but I doubt a statute like the one that passed the House would have been held to be a bill of attainder. Some members of Congress were certainly concerned about the constitutionality of the proposed tax, as were some commentators, but the Court has traditionally been lenient in allowing Congress to do all sorts of things with its tax laws. There's also a strong argument that the tax would have served the primary function of giving money back to the taxpayers, rather than of punishing anybody. The challengers' best argument, had the issue ever gone to court, would have been that Congress *intended* to punish AIG and its employees, as evidenced by statements made by specific members of the legislature (like Senator Grassley's dim observation that employees should "go commit suicide"). But as some commentators observed, once the whole bill of attainder issue started floating around, members of Congress became a lot more careful in what they said about the purpose of taxing the bonuses, changing their tune from punishment to taxpayer protection. As such, very few (if any) constitutional experts actually thought that taxing the bonuses would be found illegal. Even big pro-private-property libertarians like Richard Epstein of the New York University Law School, who wrote that "any sensible system of limited government" would find the tax proposals unconstitutional, conceded that because of the breadth of the class targeted by the bills and the deference given by the courts to Congress in tax matters, the bill-of-attainder-clause challenge would have resulted in: "No luck."

Unlike the AIG and Military Commission Act scenarios, the case involving ACORN did go to court. In 2009 a district court judge in New York struck down the law excluding ACORN from federal programs as an unconstitutional bill of attainder, but in 2010 the Second Circuit Court of Appeals reversed and upheld the law. Both courts went through the three-factor test for punishment, but they came to completely different conclusions. The district court found no "valid, non-punitive purpose" for the anti-ACORN law and was put off by some of the anti-ACORN sentiment voiced on the Senate floor, like the one senator who said: "Somebody has to go after ACORN. Madam President, I suggest this afternoon that 'somebody' is each and every Member of the Senate." The court of appeals, however, while conceding that a number of congressmen and -women had said mean things about ACORN during debate and discussion, was not willing to find a punitive intent on the basis of a "smattering" of comments from a "handful of legislators." The circuit court found that cutting an organization off from discretionary funds was not something that had historically been considered punishment. Putting this finding together with its belief that the law had been motivated by a concern for taxpayer dollars rather than by a thirst for punishment, the reviewing court found that this was not a bill of attainder.

In the *Brown* case, the Supreme Court observed that the bill of attainder clause, a "bulwark against tyranny," "was intended not as a narrow, technical (and therefore soon to be outmoded) prohibition, but rather as an implementation of the separation of powers, a general safeguard against legislative exercise of the judicial function, or more simply—trial by legislature." I've used the clause as an illustration of how the Constitution protects liberty, but I could just as easily have used it to illustrate separation of powers, or even, for that matter, congressional powers. The Constitution is an interconnected document, both in its particular provisions and its broad themes. We've seen examples of this interconnectedness throughout the book. Is the original-jurisdiction clause about judicial power, or states' rights? Are the title of nobility clauses about executive power, or equality? Speaking of equality, are the clauses setting out qualifications for public office primarily about that value, or are they about promoting democracy? Of course, the answer to each of these questions is both. Constitutional clauses, odd or not, serve several purposes and hold the document (and thus the government) together as an organic whole. In this way, the Constitution is much like the world's web of ecosystems, which the ecologists will tell you are all intertwined and intermingled in complicated and important ways. Eradicate one species here and see what happens to all sorts of other species somewhere else. It's enough to make one wonder: dear sweet Mother of God, will these analogies to the animal kingdom never end?

CHAPTER 10

The Third Amendment

Privacy

No Soldier shall, in time of peace be quartered in any
house, without the consent of the Owner, nor in time
of war, but in a manner to be prescribed by law.

Amendment III

Imagine if this happened. Some years from now, an increas-
ingly liberal population leans on its state legislatures to call
a constitutional convention as outlined in Article V of our
founding document. At the so-called Second Continental
Congress of 2024, delegates to the convention repeal the
Second Amendment and rewrite the First Amendment to
protect only "commonly agreed upon views and assertions
that are in the judgment of the community constructive."
Also, the delegates enact a new constitutional provision
making it illegal to smoke cigarettes or cigars. To reassure
some of the old constitutionalists present at the convention,
however, and to ensure the smooth passage of their preferred
reforms, the delegates decide to retain the Third Amendment, regarding the quartering of troops, even though that
clause has not played an actively prominent role in nearly
two hundred years.

About twenty-five years after the convention, a few states in the southern and southwestern part of the country decide they've had enough with this new republic and declare that they will secede. Violence breaks out in connection with this "Second Secession," and to put down the rebellion, the defense secretary and the Joint Chiefs convince the president to send troops to some of these states, including Florida and Texas. Chaos and skirmishing ensue, and in the midst of all this skirmishing and chaos, the troops decide that the spacious mansions found in the suburbs of southern cities would make perfect military headquarters. The troop commanders order the families who live in these mansions out of their homes (the lucky ones get to live in a basement corner) and move their troops in for the duration of the skirmishing. Would the ousted families have a cause of action against the military under the Third Amendment? Would it matter if Congress passed a law allowing the troops to move in?

Now, you should know that this is not a scenario that I just made up. Actually, Peggy Noonan made it up. Noonan is a former Reagan aide and high-profile conservative who writes for the *Wall Street Journal* and happens to think that the Third Amendment might prove significant some day. If I had made up the scenario, it would have been a little different. The population would have leaned right; the scrapped amendments at the convention would have been the Fourth and Eighth; and the seceding states would have been crowded up toward the Northeast. Instead of cigars and cigarettes, my convention would have banned National Public Radio and compassion. But the issue would have been the same—might there be some future set of circumstances when the Third Amendment becomes once again a critical bulwark of our right to privacy, even if the claimants turn out to be Manhattan loft-dwellers and Boston brownstone owners instead of southern suburbanites?

享

Some of the most high-profile and controversial cases ever decided by the Supreme Court have involved the constitutional right to privacy. When the Court decided in the 1965 landmark case of *Griswold v. Connecticut* that a state could not make it illegal to use contraception, it said that the challenged law was "repulsive to the notions of privacy surrounding the marriage relationship." When the Court extended *Griswold* to strike down a Massachusetts law prohibiting the distribution of contraceptives to unmarried people in *Eisenstadt v. Baird* seven years later, it said that "if the right to privacy means anything, it is the right of the *individual,* married or single, to be free from unwarranted governmental intrusion into matters so fundamentally affecting a person as the decision whether to bear or beget a child." The following year, when the Court decided *Roe v. Wade,* it observed that "the right of privacy . . . is broad enough to encompass a woman's decision whether or not to terminate her pregnancy." And when the Court held in the 2003 case of *Lawrence v. Texas* that a state may not make it illegal for two adult men to engage in anal sex, it concluded that "the petitioners are entitled to respect for their private lives" and that Texas could not "demean their existence or control their destiny by making their private sexual conduct a crime."

So here's a quiz: Where does the Constitution mention the right to privacy? Is it in the original document? The Bill of Rights? Somewhere else? Feel free at this point to fire up the Internet, take a look at the Constitution, and see if you can find it.

What? You say that you can't find it anywhere? Surely you must be mistaken. Is it possible that the Supreme Court has based some of its most important and controversial decisions on a right that isn't even mentioned in the Constitution?

You're not mistaken. It's true. Sort of.

In fact, the Court has struggled to figure out exactly where this right to privacy is actually located. To understand this struggle, it's necessary to go back to the early twentieth century, when the Supreme Court began employing an oxymoronic doctrine called "substantive due process" (linger on that phrase for a minute, soak up its absurdity) to strike down a series of laws enacted by progressive legislatures to protect the health, safety, and economic rights of workers. It all started with a 1905 case called *Lochner v. New York,* where the Court invalidated a state law setting maximum working hours for bakers to protect them from, among other things, inhaling flour dust for fifteen hours a day and contracting all sorts of awful lung diseases. The majority of the Court thought that New York's law was an unreasonable and unnecessary interference with the right of individuals to enter into contracts. Since there is no clause in the Constitution explicitly protecting the right to enter freely into contracts, however, the Court decided to make up the right and stick it into the "due process" clauses of the Fifth and Fourteenth amendments, even though those clauses quite clearly concern the *process* by which the government may deprive one of his or her liberty, and not the *substance* of what that liberty actually entails.

For the next thirty or so years, the Court, led by a group of old-guy conservatives like Willis Van Devanter and the bigot James McReynolds (two guys who, believe me, you would not want on your Supreme Court fantasy team), struck down a series of pro-employee and pro-worker laws using the substantive-due-process doctrine. It was only when FDR got sick of these guys and threatened to pack the Court full of justices who supported his New Deal policies that the Court backed down and abandoned the doctrine. In 1937 swing justice Owen Roberts decided to join the Court's liberals to uphold a minimum-wage law from the State of Washington in a case called *West Coast Hotel Company v.*

Parrish, thus bringing an end to the so-called *Lochner* era. These days, the *Lochner* era is widely reviled by constitutional scholars and historians and is generally understood as an age when the Supreme Court lost its collective mind.

Now speed up to the 1960s, when the Court was deciding *Griswold,* the Connecticut contraception case. Most of the Court thought that the law was an unconstitutional violation of individual privacy, but since privacy is not mentioned in the Constitution, the justices had to figure out just what constitutional provision the law violated. Most judges at this point wanted to avoid returning to the discredited substantive-due-process doctrine of the *Lochner* era, so they looked to places other than the due process clauses. Justice Goldberg, writing for three justices, concluded that the law violated the Ninth Amendment, a super-odd clause (though not in the sense of "odd" that I've been using) that says: "The enumeration in the Constitution, of certain rights, shall not be construed to deny or disparage others retained by the people." No justice, before or since, has seriously relied on the Ninth Amendment for anything at all. Justice Douglas, writing for the Court, came up with a different idea. According to Douglas, the right to privacy is sort of like a ghost shimmering off of the auras of a bunch of different constitutional clauses. One of those clauses is the Third Amendment: *No Soldier shall, in time of peace be quartered in any house, without the consent of the Owner, nor in time of war, but in a manner to be prescribed by law.* Here is his famous paragraph:

> The foregoing cases suggest that specific guarantees in the Bill of Rights have penumbras, formed by emanations from those guarantees that help give them life and substance. . . . Various guarantees create zones of privacy. The right of association contained in the penumbra of the First Amendment is one, as we have seen. The Third Amendment in its prohibi-

tion against the quartering of soldiers "in any house" in time of peace without the consent of the owner is another facet of that privacy. The Fourth Amendment explicitly affirms the "right of the people to be secure in their persons, houses, papers, and effects, against unreasonable searches and seizures." The Fifth Amendment in its Self-Incrimination Clause enables the citizen to create a zone of privacy which government may not force him to surrender to his detriment. The Ninth Amendment provides: "The enumeration in the Constitution, of certain rights, shall not be construed to deny or disparage others retained by the people."... The present case, then, concerns a relationship lying within the zone of privacy created by several fundamental constitutional guarantees.

Notice how this passage sounds more like it is describing a haunted house from *Scooby-Doo* than the US Constitution. Eeeek, it's the emanation of the penumbra of the Third Amendment—*Has anyone seen Shaggy?!* The inherent ridiculousness of Douglas's argument no doubt explains why, by the time the Court decided *Roe v. Wade* in 1973, it opted for the lesser of the two sillinesses and grounded the right of reproductive freedom in the same place where the Court had located the reviled right to contract sixty years earlier—in the "substantive" portion of the due process clauses. If you have never understood why even some very hard-core liberal constitutional experts think that *Roe* rests on shaky constitutional ground (Ruth Bader Ginsburg, for instance, has never been a big fan of *Roe,* and John Hart Ely once said that the decision "is not constitutional law and gives almost no sense of an obligation to try to be"), this is one reason why.

౷

The Third Amendment's brief appearance in *Griswold*—as but one small part of an argument quickly abandoned by the Court as absurd—turns out to be the provision's high point over the past two hundred years or so. This is not to say, however, that the Third Amendment was always a clause with second-class constitutional status. To the contrary, the framers thought the protection afforded to homeowners by the Third Amendment was among the most important provided by the Bill of Rights. Indeed, controversy over British quartering of troops was a key factor leading up to the Revolution itself.

The practice of quartering troops in England and a few other places in Europe goes back at least to the eleventh century, and efforts to resist it appear to reach back almost as far. The twelfth century charters of a number of important cities and towns in the United Kingdom, including London's, prohibited the "billeting" of troops in private homes. Controversy over quartering in England heated up considerably in the seventeenth century. When James II was removed from the throne in the Glorious Revolution of 1689, his removal was justified in part by his refusal to adhere to Parliament's 1679 Anti-Quartering Act. Following the ascension of William III, Parliament passed the Mutiny Act, which explicitly prohibited the billeting of troops in private homes without consent.

Meanwhile, in the Colonies, English troops had been quartering in private homes since at least the 1670s. This, understandably, led to tensions and occasional violence, which accelerated during the French and Indian War of the 1750s and '60s. In 1765 Parliament passed the Quartering Act. That act required the Colonies to provide barracks and supplies for English soldiers and further provided that if such barracks did not exist, soldiers were to be housed in "inns, livery stables, ale houses, victualling houses and the houses of sellers of wine by retail to be drank in their own houses or places thereunto belonging, and all houses of persons selling of rum, brandy, strong water, cyder or metheglin. . . ." Finally if there weren't even enough inns, livery stables, or metheglin-serving victualling houses left for the troops, the soldiers were allowed to take shelter in private buildings like uninhabited houses, outhouses, or barns. To help fund the Quartering Act's requirements, Parliament passed the Stamp Act of 1765, a law that led to the Boston Tea Party eight years later.

Once the colonists dumped tea into Boston Harbor, the road to revolution was a short one, fueled in no small part by the quartering issue. England responded to the Tea Party with five laws (the "Intolerable Acts"), including the second Quartering Act of 1774, which allowed troops to take shelter not just in unoccupied homes and outhouses, but in occupied private homes as well. Two years later, when the colonists issued the Declaration of Independence, they included the practice of troop quartering as one of their many grievances, complaining of George III's "quartering large bodies of armed troops among us." It was no surprise to anyone that after the war, a number of states included antiquartering provisions in their own laws and that when the framers finally got around to drafting a bill of rights, the antiquartering clause was right near the top of the list.

Have troops ever been quartered in private homes in violation of the Third Amendment? According to Tom Bell, now a professor at the Chapman University School of Law and author of probably the most comprehensive treatment of the Third Amendment ever written, the answer is yes—troops were quartered during both the War of 1812 and the Civil War. With respect to the quartering of troops in Union states during the Civil War, Bell explains that: "Not only are there specific reports of troops having been quartered in Union territory, but the Secretary of War alluded

to having seized the homes of loyal citizens to use as barracks. The practice grew so common that the military developed a sophisticated system for reviewing claims 'for rent for
houses . . . seized and occupied by the military authorities in
loyal States during the rebellion.'" Looking at records of the
congressional committee that oversaw these kinds of claims,
Bell reports that there were potentially "very many millions"
of dollars of claims stemming from quartering practices during the Civil War, although it appears that Congress never
actually paid any of them.

The Third Amendment has basically been hibernating for
most of its existence. For the most part the courts have not
had to deal with the amendment at all. There are a few exceptions. In 2001 a federal appellate court in Denver rejected
the argument that military aircraft training in the skies over
a plaintiff's property violated the plaintiff's Third Amendment rights, saying that the argument "borders on frivolous."
In other cases, claims have gone over the border to frivolous-
land. In one from 1972, some military reservists said that the
secretary of defense had violated their Third Amendment
rights by forcing them to march in a parade that would promote the candidacy of Spiro Agnew. The court dismissed the
argument as "inapposite," which was unsurprising, given that
a parade is not a house.

Only one court case in the history of the Republic has
actually raised a real Third Amendment issue. That case,
decided by the federal Second Circuit Court of Appeals in
New York in 1982, was called *Engblom v. Carey*. About forty
prison guards employed by the Mid-Orange Correctional
Facility in Warwick, New York, lived in employee housing
on the facility's grounds. When correction officers across the
state went on strike, the state evicted the officers from their

prison housing and used the rooms to house members of the National Guard who had been brought in to replace the striking employees. The court said that this was a violation of the Third Amendment. The state had argued that since the guards were tenants rather than owners of their housing, the amendment did not apply. The court disagreed, borrowing from case law under the more popular Fourth Amendment and finding that the employees had a substantial enough expectation of privacy in their rented housing to be able to claim protection under the Third Amendment. In further proceedings, however, the court found that individual state officials would not be liable for money damages to the displaced employees. Under the settled legal doctrine of "qualified immunity," damages (as opposed to an injunction) are only available if government officials violate a "clearly established right." Since nobody had ever previously held that anyone had ever violated anyone's Third Amendment rights, the court found that the rights of the employees violated by the state officials, while real, had not been "clearly established" so as to entitle the plaintiffs to any money. Next time, however, the officials will probably not be so lucky.

Engblom v. Carey aside, commentators have largely treated the Third Amendment as either an irrelevancy or a joke. As Professor Bell eloquently laments: "Pity the Third Amendment. The other amendments of the United States Constitution's Bill of Rights inspire public adoration and volumes of legal research. Meanwhile, the Third Amendment languishes in comparative oblivion. . . . Lawyers twist it to fit absurd claims, the popular press subjects it to ridicule, and academics relegate it to footnotes. Is this any way to treat a member of the Bill of Rights?" In a short piece called "Is the Third Amendment Obsolete?" Harvard's Morton Horwitz, maybe the country's leading legal historian, explains how, when he told his colleagues about his invitation to speak about the Third Amendment, many of them "sheepishly asked me what the Third Amendment is."

In the constitutional zoo, most experts would probably identify the Third Amendment as a dodo bird.

Some Third Amendment jokes are, admittedly, pretty funny. Not so much the one in a cartoon found on the ACLU's Web site, where George W. Bush decides that, like the Fourth Amendment, the Third Amendment "has to go." In the final frame of the comic strip, a soldier sitting at a family's dinner table explains "why you always do cavity searches BEFORE dinner," while the daughter asks him to "pass the gravy." Yuck. Somewhat better was the guy dressed as a British soldier at the Rally to Restore Sanity in Washington, DC, last October, holding a "Repeal the Third Amendment" sign. But the crème de la crème of Third Amendment jokes is surely the *Onion*'s article "Third Amendment Rights Group Celebrates Another Successful Year," where it is reported that the National Anti-Quartering Association ("NAQA"), whose "familiar slogan" is "Keep the fat hands of soldiers out of America's Larders!" and whose "fully staffed regional centers" are always available for citizens to "report Third Amendment abuses," has just celebrated its 191st anniversary of "advocating the protection of private homes and property against the unlawful boarding of military personnel." The article, which I would print in full here if it weren't for the "copyright laws," ends by explaining that the group's new president replaced its former leader, who had recently "left the organization to chair the Citizens Committee for the Right to Drink, a 21st Amendment rights group committed to the continued legal status of alcohol for Americans of drinking age."

Does the *Onion* have a book review section?

Will the Third Amendment ever regain the fame enjoyed by its well-known brothers and sisters in the Bill of Rights? Before I get to that question, it is worth pointing out that if you think about it for a while, you might conclude that the Third Amendment has in fact done a better job than any of its neighbors. The article in the *Onion* is obviously meant to be funny, but I think there is something serious to be said for the fact that the government has not quartered any troops in private homes for at least the past 145 years. Just because the Third Amendment hasn't come up much doesn't mean that it hasn't done any work. Maybe the amendment isn't hibernating at all. Maybe it is more accurate to say that it is just quietly doing its job, making it simply impossible to imagine under current circumstances that the army or National Guard or any other military organization could take shelter in private homes. Who knows how our history might have been different were it not for the Third Amendment? Maybe the government would have adopted a policy of quartering troops very early on, and maybe as a result that policy would seem so natural today that we wouldn't even question it. I mean, people rarely think about plankton, and plankton would never be a popular zoo exhibit even though some plankton are in fact animals and not plants (zooplankton, specifically), but that doesn't mean that plankton aren't doing an important job—they essentially sustain our massive ocean ecosystems. Perhaps we shouldn't make fun of the Third Amendment any more than we should make fun of plankton, which means that we should make fun of it once in a while, sure, but not too often.

On the question of fame, though, there are two ways that the Third Amendment could rise to prominence. One way is for the courts to start interpreting the clause to apply to situations far beyond what the language of the amendment would seem to suggest. This would hardly be the first time that courts have done such a thing—think about the *Lochner* era, for instance, or our modern right to privacy, which I just talked about like eight pages ago. Usually when courts do this, they do what the scholars we met back in chapter 5 suggested they might do with respect to the requirement that you have to be at least thirty-five years old to become president. They find that the clause represents a broad principle rather than simply being limited to the specific stuff that is pointed to by the language. Thus, courts have interpreted the bill of attainder clause, as we saw in chapter 9, to prohibit all legislative punishments rather than only legislatively-imposed death penalties involving awful things being done to one's privy-parts. Or, as we saw back in chapter 6, the Supreme Court has interpreted the Tenth Amendment, whose language hardly suggests anything at all, to bar the federal government from commandeering the administrative apparatus or employees of the states.

Unfortunately for the Third Amendment, no court has yet seen fit to apply the clause to anything beyond the straightforward quartering of troops in private homes. Perhaps this is because the language of the clause is so very specific, or perhaps it is because the Fourth Amendment, with its prohibition of unreasonable searches and seizures, already covers the kinds of things that courts might have extended the Third Amendment to cover. Or, then again, perhaps it is because nobody has ever made a plausible creative argument before a court on behalf of the beleaguered amendment. On this latter point, however, some scholars have at least tried to come up with something to resurrect the clause, even if these theories have thus far merely graced the pages of academic journals rather than court documents.

One spirited writer, for example, has argued that the Third Amendment stands for the principle that civil power should always be superior to military power in times of peace. He writes: "The Third Amendment establishes an explicit limit to the military's power, vesting a right in the individual that, at least textually, appears to be absolute in times of peace. In this sense, the Third Amendment stands alone as a constitutional provision that reflects the judgment that at least one peacetime right will always trump military necessity no matter what form it takes."The writer goes on to argue that the Third Amendment, interpreted in this broad fashion, prohibited the federal government from requiring private universities to allow the military, with its "don't ask, don't tell" policy for gays and lesbians, access to campuses for recruiting purposes, if the universities wanted to continue to receive certain federal funds. Similarly, another writer has argued that the Third Amendment establishes "a categorical ban on soldiers enforcing law against civilians in all areas in which private citizens may exclude others." Applying this principle, the author argues that the amendment places substantial limits on the federal government's power to intercept through wiretapping the "communications of individuals living in the United States." According to this theory, officials of the National Security Agency are "soldiers," and their wiretapping counts as "quartering." Finally, two professors have argued in a prominent environmental law journal that the Endangered Species Act, by requiring private landowners to "quarter" endangered species on their property, violates the Third Amendment. It turns out, however, that the article is a forty-one-page satire that pokes fun both at the act and the method of constitutional interpretation that would extend constitutional provisions beyond their plain language.

The other way, of course, that the Third Amendment might rise to prominence is if our current, relatively peaceful situation here in the United States were to change radically. In some new, highly dangerous situation, one could easily imagine circumstances under which the military might find it advantageous to quarter its troops in private homes. Peggy Noonan's hypothetical that started the chapter (and my lefty permutation of her scenario) is one example, but hardly the only one. Noonan herself, for instance, suggests one more: "Suppose that down the road there is a nuclear or biological or chemical incident in, say, downtown Manhattan. The island is quarantined; in time there is civil unrest; in time the 101st Airborne comes in to restore the peace. Where do they live in this chaotic and uncontrolled environment as they realize they must occupy the island? Perhaps among the people. The government condemns their property and seizes it." I'm sure you can think of others. The world is filled with dangers—not just terrorism and civil unrest but also diseases, plagues, chemical explosions, earthquakes, tidal waves, killer bees, and who knows what else—all of which could lead to the military playing a more involved role in the daily life of citizens. If there's no clear place where the soldiers would obviously stay (particularly possible if, for instance, an earthquake has knocked down the obvious place, or if killer bees have already taken up residence there), then the issue of quartering troops in private homes becomes a distinct possibility.

The notion that the military might want to house troops in private homes during times of crisis, rather than in times of outright war, raises some interesting legal issues. Indeed, although Noonan implies with her hypothetical that the Third Amendment would save homeowners from forced quartering in the case of civil rebellion, it is not entirely clear that that's the case. Look at the specific language of the Third Amendment. In "time of peace," quartering is unconstitutional unless the owner consents. In "time of war," however, quartering is unconstitutional unless done "in a manner to be prescribed by law," which means that if we are in a time of war, Congress can pass a law authorizing the quartering of troops. But what counts as a "time of war"? Does the "war" referred to in the Third Amendment mean only "war" declared by Congress under Article I—something we saw in chapter 7 that has only happened five times in history? Or might it also apply to something short of formally declared "war," and if so, what? Moreover, if "war" does mean only formally declared war, then what happens if there's no formal declaration of war but we're not in a time of peace, either? Since the amendment seems silent on that question, might the president be allowed to order quartering under those circumstances? Perhaps someday a scenario like Noonan's will arise and the Supreme Court will be called on to decide these issues. It would be a fascinating constitutional case, but let's hope it never comes to that.

So, the Third Amendment? It's probably the clause in the Constitution that people make fun of the most (the slavery portions are too distressing to make real fun of), but is it really a constitutional dodo bird? Maybe, as I've suggested, it's better to think of it as plankton. Or perhaps, as Noonan reminds us, the Third Amendment could turn out to be a coelacanth. The coelacanth is a huge bottom-dwelling fish with a teeny-tiny brain that looks kind of like a science fiction monster and that was extremely common hundreds of millions of years ago. Having never seen a live one before, scientists had long thought coelacanths had gone extinct along with the dinosaurs at the end of the Cretaceous period, but then a museum curator discovered one swimming near the Chalumna River off the South African coast in 1938. Since then, coelacanths have been found as far away from Africa as Saint Lucia and Indonesia.

One of the best quotes I found while doing research on this book comes from a judge on the Sixth Circuit Court of Appeals named Martha Craig Daughtrey, who, in a dissent responding to the court majority's argument that some provision of the tax code was unimportant because the IRS hadn't litigated a case involving it in the twenty-two years since it was enacted, made this point about the completely unrelated Third Amendment: ·

Clearly, such a lack of litigation bears no necessary correlation to the importance of the subject matter. As recognized by our sister circuit, for example, in the 216 years since the adoption of the Third Amendment to the United States Constitution, "[j]udicial interpretation of [that provision] is nearly nonexistent." . . . The Third Amendment's prohibition on the quartering of soldiers in private residences without consent is, however, one of the constitutional bulwarks protecting privacy rights inherent in American citizenship. Especially in this time of seemingly unfettered governmental efforts to intrude into private realms, I would hope that the majority would not equate the "nearly nonexistent" litigation involving the Third Amendment with a lack of importance of the principles protected by that provision.

Judge Daughtrey's point about the Third Amendment not being irrelevant just because it never gets litigated is broadly relevant to the odd clauses that I've discussed in this book. These clauses rarely make it anywhere near a courtroom. As Judge Daughtrey suggests, though, you can't always judge a provision by its visibility. The Constitution's odd clauses—whether they are giving power to the three branches of government or keeping the branches separate or protecting the liberty, privacy, and equality of the citizens governed by those branches—are well worth our attention, even if hardly anybody has ever heard of them, until now.

Okay, the constitutional zoo is now getting ready to close. Thank you so much for coming. Please exit through the gift shop.

Acknowledgments

I would like to thank the faculties at the Boston University School of Law, the Saint Louis University School of Law, and the University of Colorado School of Law for helpful discussions about this book and comments on drafts of various chapters, as well as the following supergreat individuals who helped me so much and without whom this book would not exist: Helene Atwan, Mark Dahl, Ellen Geiger, Carlos Maycotte, Michael O'Malley, Maureen O'Rourke, Karen Tokos, Caitlin Meyer, Allison Trzop, Paz Valencia, Fred Wexler, Mary Wexler, and Walter Wexler.

Notes

For general reading about the Constitution, I recommend the following: Akhil Reed Amar, *America's Constitution: A Biography* (New York: Random House, 2006); Akhil Reed Amar, *The Bill of Rights: Creation and Reconstruction* (New Haven, CT: Yale University Press, 1998); Erwin Chemerinsky, *Constitutional Law: Principles and Policies* (New York: Aspen, 2006); and Laurence H. Tribe, *American Constitutional Law*, 3rd ed. (New York: Foundation, 2000).

CHAPTER 1: THE INCOMPATIBILITY CLAUSE

The best overall account of the incompatibility clause is Steven G. Calabresi and Joan L. Larsen, "One Person, One Office: Separation of Powers or Separation of Personnel?" *Cornell Law Review* 79, no. 5 (1994): 1045–1157 . For a nice description and defense of separation of powers generally, check out Martin H. Redish and Elizabeth J. Cisar, "'If Angels Were to Govern': The Need for Pragmatic Formalism in Separation of Powers Theory," *Duke Law Journal* 41, no. 3 (1991): 449–506. To see what the framers had to say about separation of powers, one good place to look is *The Federalist Papers*, especially nos. 47, 48, and 51. The case where the Court held that Congress could not reserve to itself the right to veto the president's firing of an executive officer is Myers v. United

States, 272 U.S. 52 (1926). The case where the Court approved of a statute creating the independent counsel is Morrison v. Olson, 487 U.S. 654 (1988). The phrase "bankrupts, bullies, and blockheads," is reported from Calabresi and Larsen's "One Person, One Office," p. 1057, which itself quotes from the classic historical work Gordon S. Wood, *The Creation of the American Republic, 1776–1787* (1969), which in turn quotes a March 26, 1778, issue of the *Boston Independent Chronicle*. For the debate over whether the president must step down from a congressional seat upon taking the oath of office, see the following: Seth Barrett Tillman, "Why Our Next President May Keep His or Her Senate Seat: A Conjecture on the Constitution's Incompatibility Clause," *Duke Journal of Constitutional Law & Public Policy* 4 (2009): 107–41; Saikrishna Bangalore Prakash, "Why the Incompatibility Clause Applies to the Office of the President," *Duke Journal of Constitutional Law & Public Policy* 4 (2009): 143–51. For the lower federal-court case on the military reservists, see Reservists Committee to Stop War v. Laird, 323 F. Supp 833 (1971). For the Supreme Court case, see Schlesinger v. Reservists Committee to Stop the War, 418 U.S. 208 (1974). For historical discussions of the executive branch's meandering interpretation of the ineligibility clause, see Daniel H. Pollitt, "Senator/Attorney-General Saxbe and the 'Ineligibility Clause' of the Constitution: An Encroachment Upon Separation of Powers," *North Carolina Law Review* 53, no. 1 (1974): 111–33, and Michael Stokes Paulsen, "Is Lloyd Bentsen Unconstitutional?" *Stanford Law Review* 46, no. 4 (1994): 907–18. For the last two OLC opinions on the ineligibility clause, see Memorandum Opinion for the Attorney General from David J. Barron, Acting Assistant Attorney General, "Validity of Statutory Rollbacks as a Means of Complying with the Ineligibility Clause," May 20, 2009, available on the Web site of the Office of Legal Counsel, www.justice.gov/olc/. The Cooper memorandum on Orrin Hatch had not previously been released until the release of the May 2009 memorandum, although at least one scholar—Michael Paulsen, whose aforementioned piece on Lloyd Bentsen is a fascinating and entertaining read that I rely on for the story about Bork, Hatch, and Kennedy—had suspected that such a memorandum existed. Paulsen speculates that if it weren't for the Reagan administration's strict adherence to the text of the ineligibility clause, perhaps *Roe v. Wade* might have been overruled, since it is unlikely that Orrin Hatch would have joined any sort of opinion upholding the earlier case, as Justice Anthony Kennedy did in the case *Planned Parenthood v. Casey* in 1992. The two commentators who think the incompatibility clause is responsible for keeping our government from becoming parliamentary-like are Calabresi and Larsen, cited above. To read the views of the separation-of-powers critics, see Donald L. Robinson, ed., *Reforming American Government: The Bicentennial Papers of the Committee on the Constitutional System* (Boulder, CO: Westview, 1985). To read an excellent critique of these views, see Thomas O. Sargentich, "The Limits of the Parliamentary Critique of the Separation of Powers," *William and Mary Law Review* 34, no. 3 (1993): 679–739.

CHAPTER 2: THE WEIGHTS AND MEASURES CLAUSE

On the Mars climate orbiter fiasco, see the following: John Noble Wilford, "Mars Orbiting Craft Presumed Destroyed by Navigation Error," *New York Times*, September 24, 1999; Andrew Pollack, "Two Teams, Two Measures Equaled One Lost Spacecraft," *New York Times*, October 1, 1999. The case involving the California toad is Rancho Viejo, LLC v. Norton, 323 F.3d 1062 (DC Circuit 2003). The citation for *Lopez* is 514 U.S. 549 (1995). The Violence Against Women Act case is United States v. Morrison, 529 U.S. 598 (2000). The case involving medical marijuana is Gonzalez v. Raich, 545 U.S. 1 (2005). The article that suggests Congress had exercised all of its powers before it ever exercised its weights and measures power is David P. Currie, "Weights and Measures," *Green Bag* 2, no. 3 (1999): 261–66. This article also discusses the early history of the weights and measures clause, including the various commissioned reports of Jefferson and Adams. The report of the academic committee from New York, which includes Adams's famous report, is Charles L. Davies, *The Metric System, Considered with Reference to Its Introduction into the United States; Embracing the Reports of the Hon. John Quincy Adams, and the Lecture of Sir John Herschel* (New York and Chicago: A. S. Barnes & Co., 1871). For the story about how the official kilogram is shedding a tiny bit of its weight every year, see Otto Pohl, "Scientists Struggling to Make the Kilogram Right Again," *New York Times*, May 27, 2003. For a history of the United States Metric Board, see United States Metric Association, *History of the United States Metric Board*, http://lamar.colostate.edu/~hillger/laws/usmb.html. Also see David Bjerklie, "What Ever Happened to Metric?" *Time*, July 6, 1987. For the most recent case on the "intelligible principle" doctrine, see Whitman v. American Trucking Association, 531 U.S. 457 (2001). For Mankiewicz's account of his conspiracy with Nofziger to get rid of the Metric Board, see Frank Mankiewicz, "Nofziger: A Friend with Whom It Was a Pleasure to Disagree," *Washington Post*, March 29, 2006.

CHAPTER 3: THE RECESS-APPOINTMENTS CLAUSE

The controversial appointee who was accused of being racially insensitive was Charles Pickering. For more on his nomination, see Neil A. Lewis, "Bush Seats Judge after Long Fight, Bypasses Senate Democrats," *New York Times*, January 17, 2004. The judge who was proud of ruling against children with birth defects was Priscilla Owens. For more on her nomination, see David D. Kirkpatrick, "For Judge Owen, Self-Reliance in Life and Law," *New York Times*, May 26, 2005. On Pryor, see Sheryl Gay Stolberg, "A Different Timpanist," *New York Times*, June 10, 2005. The following are excellent academic articles on the recess-appointments clause; I relied on these sources for much of my discussion of the clause, its history, and the issues it has raised: Edward A. Hartnett, "Recess Appointments of Article III Judges: Three Constitutional Questions," *Cardozo Law Review* 26, no. 2 (2005): 377–442; Michael Herz, "Abandoning Recess Appointments? A Comment on Hartnett (and Others)," *Cardozo Law Review* 26, no. 2 (2005): 443–62; and Michael B. Rappaport, "The Original Meaning of the Recess Appointments Clause," *UCLA Law Review* 52, no. 5 (2005): 1487–1578. Another excellent source of information is Henry B. Hogue, *CRS Report for Congress—Recess Appointments: Frequently Asked Questions* (Washington, DC: Congressional Research Service, 2008). The commentator who talks about vacations as "happening" is Hartnett, "Recess Appointments of Article III

Judges," at pp. 382–83. The *New York Times* editorial was published on December 8, 1903. The Knox opinion is "President—Appointment of Officers—Holiday Recess," *Official Opinions of the Attorney General of the United States* 23 (December 24, 1901). The Daugherty opinion is "Executive Power—Recess Appointments," *Official Opinions of the Attorney General of the United States* 33 (August 27, 1921). The opinion about public committees starting off their sessions with sectarian prayers is Pelphrey v. Cobb County, 547 F.3d 1263 (11th Cir. 2008). On the issue of whether the Senate can terminate the president's recess appointments, see Seth Barrett Tillman, "Senate Termination of Presidential Recess Appointments," *Northwestern University Law Review Colloquy* 103 (January 2009): 286–91, and Brian Kalt, "Keeping Recess Appointments in Their Place," *Northwestern University Law Colloquy* 103 (January 2009): 292–97. These two have written other articles on the subject, but I'll spare you. Kalt's article about Idaho is "The Perfect Crime," *Georgetown Law Journal* 93, no. 2 (2005): 675–88. The court of appeals decision in the Pryor case is Evans v. Stephens, 387 F.3d 1220 (11th Cir. 2004).

CHAPTER 4: THE ORIGINAL-JURISDICTION CLAUSE

The Ellis Island case is New Jersey v. New York, 523 U.S. 767 (1998). The case where a federal appellate court ruled that New York law applied on the island is Collins v. Promark Products, 956 F.2d 383 (2nd Cir. 1992). The "judicial review" case is Marbury v. Madison, 5 U.S. (1 Cranch) 137 (1803). The statute that gives district courts concurrent jurisdiction over most of the types of cases that fall under the Supreme Court's original jurisdiction is 28 U.S.C. § 1251. The most comprehensive source for information about state-versus-state cases, and a book on which I draw heavily for my information and categorization of the various cases, is Joseph F. Zimmerman, *Interstate Disputes: The Supreme Court's Original Jurisdiction* (Albany: State University of New York, 2006). Cites for all of the state-versus-state cases discussed in the chapter can be found in Zimmerman's book, but here are citations for a few of the cases discussed here: Texas v. Florida, 306 U.S. 398 (1939); New Mexico v. Texas, 275 U.S. 279 (1927); Missouri v. Illinois, 200

U.S. 496 (1906). The *Time* magazine article about the Maine–New Hampshire dispute is "New England: Lobster War," July 2, 1973. The best source of information about the special masters is Anne-Marie C. Carstens, "Lurking in the Shadows of Judicial Process: Special Masters in the Supreme Court's Original Jurisdiction Cases," *Minnesota Law Review* 86, no. 3 (2001): 625–716. Other articles on the original-jurisdiction clause include James Pfander, "Rethinking the Supreme Court's Original Jurisdiction in State-Party Cases," *California Law Review* 82, no. 3 (1994): 555–662; and "The Original Jurisdiction of the United States Supreme Court," *Stanford Law Review* 11 (July 1959): 665–700. A short and funny piece on Supreme Court jury trials is Robert A. James, "Instructions in Supreme Court Jury Trials," *Green Bag* 1, no. 4 (1998): 377–80.

CHAPTER 5: THE NATURAL-BORN CITIZEN CLAUSE

The symposium put together by William Eskridge and Sanford Levinson is called "Constitutional Stupidities: A Symposium," *Constitutional Commentary* 12, no. 2 (1995): 139–225. The symposium was later turned into a book: William N. Eskridge and Sanford Levinson, eds., *Constitutional Stupidities, Constitutional Tragedies* (New York: New York University Press, 1998). The point about getting no points for condemning the fugitive slave law was made by Lief Carter, "'Clause and Effect': An Imagined Conversation with Sanford Levinson," *Constitutional Commentary* 12, no. 2 (1995): 155–58. The professor who called the symposium "vapid" was Phillip Bobbitt, "Parlor Game," *Constitutional Commentary* 12, no. 2 (1995): 151–54. The critic of life tenure who likened the United States to China was L. A. Powe Jr., "Old People and Good Behavior," *Constitutional Commentary* 12, no. 2 (1995): 195–97. The two articles criticizing the natural-born citizen clause in the symposium were Randall Kennedy, "A Natural Aristocracy?" *Constitutional Commentary* 12, no. 2 (1995): 175–77, and Robert Post, "What Is the Constitution's Worst Provision?" *Constitutional Commentary* 12, no. 2 (1995): 191–93. Post is the one who called the clause a "vestigial excrescence." The case holding term limits unconstitutional is U.S. Term Limits, Inc. v. Thornton, 514

U.S. 779 (1995). On the age requirement for president, the case in which Frankfurter noted that it "draws on arithmetic" is National Mutual Ins. Co. v. Tidewater Transfer Co., 337 U.S. 582, 646 (1949) (Frankfurter, J., dissenting). For the argument that "thirty-five" means sufficiently mature or experienced, see Giradeau Spann, "Deconstructing the Legislative Veto," *Minnesota Law Review* 68 (1984): 532. For the extension of that argument, see Gary Peller, "The Metaphysics of American Law," *California Law Review* 73 (1985): 1174. On the "unstoppable virus," see Anthony D'Amato, "Aspects of Deconstruction: The 'Easy Case' of the Under-Aged President," *Northwestern University Law Review* 84 (1990): 255. For the "teenage guru," see Mark Tushnet, "A Note on the Revival of Textualism in Constitutional Theory," *Southern California Law Review* 58 (1985): 686–88. For criticism of the natural-born citizen clause, see Frederick Schauer, "Constitutional Invocations," *Fordham Law Review* 65 (1997): 1301 ("morally dubious"); William Safire, "The Constitution's Flaw," *New York Times,* September 6, 1987 ("blatantly discriminatory"); John W. Dean, "The Pernicious 'Natural Born' Clause of the Constitution," *FindLaw,* Writ, October 8, 2004, http://writ.news.findlaw.com/dean/20041008.html ("lowdown dirty shame" and "inane"; "Permit me"); Post, "What Is the Constitution's Worst Provision?" ("highly objectionable"). For excellent general articles discussing the history and meaning of the natural-born citizen clause, see Jill A. Pryor, "The Natural-Born Citizen Clause and Presidential Eligibility: An Approach for Resolving Two Hundred Years of Uncertainty," *Yale Law Journal* 97, no. 5 (1988): 881–900; Christina S. Lohman, "Presidential Eligibility: The Meaning of the Natural-Born Citizen Clause," *Gonzaga Law Review* 36, no. 2 (2000–01): 349–74; and Sarah Helene Duggin and Mary Beth Collins, "'Natural Born' in the USA: The Striking Unfairness and Dangerous Ambiguity of the Constitution's Presidential Qualifications Clause and Why We Need to Fix It," *Boston University Law Review* 85, no. 1 (2005): 53–154. For the Bob Hope example, see Schauer, "Constitutional Invocations," at p. 1302, n. 28. Information about the birther movement is everywhere on the Web. For one good account, see Alex Koppelman, "Why the Stories about Obama's Birth Certificate Will Never Die," *Salon,* December 5, 2008, http://www.salon

.com/news/feature/2008/12/05/birth_certificate. On the number
of people who think Obama was born abroad, see Dalia Sussman
and Marina Stefan, "Obama and the 'Birthers' in the Latest Poll,"
New York Times, April 21, 2010. The Washington, DC, judicial
opinion is Hollister v. Soetoro, 601 F.Supp. 2d 179 (D.D.C. 2009).
The opinion from California is Barnett v. Obama (C.D. Cal. Oct.
29, 2009). The opinion from Georgia is Rhodes v. MacDonald
(M.D. Ga. Sept. 18, 2009). For Medved's comments, see Ben
Smith, "Culture of Conspiracy: The Birthers," *Politico,* March 1,
2009. For the argument about Obama being a kitten and meow-
ing all day long, see Teo Bear, "Birthers and Dualers are Constitutionalists," http://www.birthers.org/misc/birthersdualers.html
(last accessed May 26, 2010). For the Tribe-Olson memo on Mc-
Cain, see appendix A: "Opinion of Laurence H. Tribe and Theodore B. Olson Dated March 19, 2008," in Gabriel J. Chin, "Why
Senator John McCain Cannot Be President: Eleven Months and a
Hundred Yards Short of Citizenship," *Michigan Law Review First
Impressions* 107 (2008): 19–21, http://www.michiganlawreview.org/
assets/fi/107/chin.pdf. For the argument in favor of McCain responding to Chin, see Stephen E. Sachs, "Why John McCain
Was a Citizen At Birth," *Michigan Law Review First Impressions*
107 (2008): 49–57, http://www.michiganlawreview.org/assets/fi/107/
sachs.pdf. The current succession statute is located at 3 U.S.C.
§ 19. James Ho's piece is "Unnatural Born Citizens and Acting
Presidents," *Constitutional Commentary* 17, no. 3 (2000): 575–86.
Ho quotes *Demolition Man* in his footnote 10.

CHAPTER 6: THE TWENTY-FIRST AMENDMENT

The bottomless-dancing case is California v. Larue, 409 U.S. 109
(1972). Okrent's terrific book about Prohibition is Daniel Okrent,
Last Call: The Rise and Fall of Prohibition (New York: Scribner,
2010). Tribe's piece about the Twenty-first Amendment is Laurence H. Tribe, "How to Violate the Constitution without Really
Trying: Lessons from the Repeal of Prohibition to the Balanced
Budget Amendment," *Constitutional Commentary* 12 (1995): 217–21.
For the discussion of "maximalist" and "minimalist" interpreta-
tions of Section 2, see Jonathan M. Rotter and Joshua S. Stam-

baugh, "What's Left of the Twenty-first Amendment?" *Cardozo Public Law, Policy, & Ethics Journal* 6, no. 3 (2008): 601–50. The California beer tax case is State Board of Equalization v. Young's Market Co., 299 U.S. 59 (1936). The topless-dancing case is New York State Liquor Authority v. Bellanca, 452 U.S. 714 (1981). The Y chromosome 3.2 percent beer case is Craig v. Boren, 429 U.S. 190 (1976). The Rhode Island liquor-advertising case is 44 Liquormart, Inc. v. Rhode Island, 517 U.S. 484 (1996). The Court has upheld nude dancing and other adult-entertainment regulations on the grounds that these regulations target the secondary effects of the dancing, rather than the entertainment itself—see City of Renton v. Playtime Theaters, Inc., 475 U.S. 41 (1986)—or because nude dancing is conduct rather than speech, or because regulation of nude dancing is justified by moral concerns, see Barnes v. Glen Theatre, Inc., 501 U.S. 560 (1991). The Puerto Rico no-serving-alcohol-in-the-wee-hours-of-the-morning case is Broadwell v. San Juan, 312 F.Supp.2d 132 (D. Puerto Rico 2004). The Missouri pool hall case is Spudich v. Smarr, 931 F.2d 1278 (8th Cir. 1991). The Yablon-Zug piece is Marcia Yablon, "The Prohibition Hangover: Why We Are Still Feeling the Effects of Prohibition," *Virginia Journal of Social Policy & the Law* 13 (Spring 2006): 552–95. For an excellent account of what Section 2 was supposed to mean, see Asheesh Agarwal and Todd Zywicki, "The Original Meaning of the 21st Amendment," *Green Bag* 8, no. 2 (2005): 137–43. The Hawaii pineapple-wine case is Bacchus Imports, Ltd. v. Dias, 468 U.S. 263 (1984). The case striking the discriminatory Michigan and New York laws is Granholm v. Heald, 544 U.S. 460 (2005).

CHAPTER 7: THE LETTERS OF
MARQUE AND REPRISAL CLAUSE

For the full story of the *Maersk Alabama,* see Robert D. McFadden and Scott Shane, "In Rescue of Captain, Navy Kills 3 Pirates," *New York Times,* April 13, 2009, and Mark Mazzetti and Sharon Otterman, "U.S. Captain Is Hostage of Pirates; Navy Ship Arrives," *New York Times,* April 9, 2009. On Paul's suggestion to use letters of marque to fight pirates, see Erika Lovley, "Ron Paul's Plan to Fend Off Pirates," *Politico,* April 15, 2009.

For Ely's point about Congress's authority to instigate all hostilities, see John Hart Ely, *War and Responsibility: Constitutional
Lessons of Vietnam and Its Aftermath* (Princeton, NJ: Princeton
University Press, 1995). The other pro-Congress scholar quoted
is Louis Fisher, from his *Presidential War Power* (Lawrence:
University Press of Kansas, 1995). The quote from John Yoo on
presidential authority to instigate hostilities is from "The Con-
tinuation of Politics by Other Means: The Original Understanding of War Powers," *California Law Review* 84 (March 1996):
167–305. To read the "torture memo" and other related documents
from the Bush administration, take a look (if you can bear to) at
Karen J. Greenberg and Joshua L. Dratel, eds., *The Torture Papers: The Road to Abu Ghraib* (New York: Cambridge University
Press, 2005). The "dynamic duo" is David J. Barron and Martin
S. Lederman; the quote is from their article "The Commander
in Chief at the Lowest Ebb—A Constitutional History," *Harvard Law Review* 121, no. 4 (2008): 941–1111. The Prakash quote
is from Saikrishna Bangalore Prakash, "Separation and Overlap
of War and Military Powers," *Texas Law Review* 87, no. 2 (2008):
299–386. On the history of letters of marque and reprisal, see J.
Gregory Sidak, "The Quasi War Cases—and Their Relevance to
Whether 'Letters of Marque and Reprisal' Constrain Presidential
War Powers," *Harvard Journal of Law and Public Policy* 28 (Spring
2005): 465–500; C. Kevin Marshall, "Putting Privateers in Their
Place: The Applicability of the Marque and Reprisal Clause to
Undeclared Wars," *University of Chicago Law Review* 64, no. 3
(1997): 953–82; and Nicholas Parrillo, "The De-Privatization of
American Warfare: How the U.S. Government Used, Regulated,
and Ultimately Abandoned Privateering in the Nineteenth Century," *Yale Journal of Law and Humanities* 19, no. 1 (2007): 1–95.
On the relationship between the letters of marque and reprisal
clause and the president's authority (or nonauthority) to instigate
hostilities, the other "prominent writer" is Jules Lobel, "'Little
Wars' and the Constitution," *University of Miami Law Review*
50, no. 1 (1995): 61–80. The defenders of presidential powers on
this score are John Yoo and C. Kevin Marshall, in the articles
cited above. The quote from Jules Lobel on the issue of Congress's
power to make tactical decisions during wartime comes from his

article "Conflicts between the Commander in Chief and Congress: Concurrent Power over the Conduct of War," *Ohio State Law Journal* 69, no. 3 (2008): 391–467. The other article cited is Ingrid Brunk Wuerth's "International Law and Constitutional Interpretation: The Commander in Chief Clause Reconsidered," *Michigan Law Review* 106, no. 1 (2007): 61–100. The quote about Johnny Depp is from Andrew Grotto of the Center for American Progress, quoted in the *Politico* article cited above; the quote about Swiss bank accounts also comes from this article and was uttered by Eli Lehrer of the Competitive Enterprise Institute (who also is the source of the Rambo quote earlier in the chapter). The military expert whose law journal article weighs in on the letters of marque issue is Major Theodore Richard, who makes the point in "Reconsidering the Letter of Marque: Utilizing Private Security Providers against Piracy," *Public Contract Law Journal* 39, no. 3 (2010): 411–64.

CHAPTER 8: THE TITLE OF NOBILITY CLAUSES

The account of Norman Schwarzkopf's knighthood comes from Karen de Witt, "No Sword and No Kneeling, Schwarzkopf Is Knighted," *New York Times*, May 21, 1991; and Christopher Hitchens, "Knighting of General Norman Schwarzkopf," *Nation*, June 17, 1991. The Supreme Court cases described in the section on equality are Brown v. Board of Education, 347 U.S. 483 (1954); Loving v. Virginia, 388 U.S. 1 (1967); Batson v. Kentucky, 476 U.S. 79 (1986); and United States v. Virginia, 518 U.S. 515 (1996). Much of the information about the history of the title of nobility clauses comes from Carlton F. W. Larson, "Titles of Nobility, Hereditary Privilege, and the Unconstitutionality of Legacy Preferences in Public School Admissions," *Washington University Law Review* 84, no. 6 (2006): 1375–1440; and Jol A. Silversmith, "The 'Missing Thirteenth Amendment': Constitutional Nonsense and Titles of Nobility," *Southern California Interdisciplinary Law Journal* 8 (April 1999): 577. The controversy over the Society of the Cincinnati is recounted in Larson, "Titles of Nobility." I got the facts about the knighted Norwegian penguin from Raphael G. Satter/Associated Press, "King Penguin Receives Norwegian Knighthood at Scottish Zoo," ReadingEagle.com (Penn.), August 15, 2008, http://readingeagle.com/article.aspx?id=102427. The attorney general opinion about J. A. Udden is "Field Assistant on the Geological Survey—Acceptance of an Order from the King of Sweden," *Official Opinions of the Attorney General of the United States* 28 (1911). The Foreign Gifts and Decorations Act can be found at 5 U.S.C. section 7342. The information about the titles of nobility amendment comes from Silversmith, The 'Missing Thirteenth Amendment.'" For more on the Twenty-seventh Amendment, and other amendments that have never been ratified, see Richard L. Berke, "More Amendments Lurk in the Mists of History," *New York Times,* May 24, 1992. The military rank system case is United States v. Thomason, 444 F.2d 1094 (D. Cal. 1971). The magistrate case is United States v. Riley, 1991 WL 192115 (D. Kan. 1991). The driver's license case is State v. Larson, 419 N.W. 2d 897 (ND 1988). The "von" case is In re Jama, 272 N.Y.S.2d 677 (N.Y. City Civ. Ct. 1966). The article by Larson is "Titles of Nobility," cited above. The article by Liptak is Adam Liptak, "A Hereditary Perk the Founding Fathers Failed to Anticipate," *New York Times,* January 15, 2008. The article by Delgado is Richard Delgado, "Inequality 'From the Top': Applying an Ancient Prohibition to an Emerging Problem of Distributive Justice," *UCLA Law Review* 32, no. 1 (1984): 100–134.

CHAPTER 9: THE BILL OF ATTAINDER CLAUSES

On the Military Commissions Act, see Hamdan v. Gates, 565 F. Supp. 2d 130 (D.D.C. 2008), and the February 20, 2008, decision of military judge Peter E. Brownback III in United States v. Omar Ahmed Khadr. On AIG, see Carl Hulse and David Herszenhorn, "House Approves 90% Tax on Bonuses after Bailouts," *New York Times,* March 19, 2009. On the ACORN controversy, see ACORN v. United States, 662 F. Supp. 2d 585 (E.D. N.Y. 2009). On the commitment of sex offenders and the ex post facto clauses, see Smith v. Doe, 538 U.S. 84 (2003). On the bill of attainder clause generally, see the discussion in Zechariah Chafee Jr., *Three Human Rights in the Constitution of 1787* (Lawrence: University of Kansas Press, 1956), and an unsigned student article that turned out to have been written by John Hart Ely, "The Bounds of Legislative Specification: A Suggested Approach to the Bill of Attainder Clause," *Yale Law Journal* 72, no. 2 (1962): 330–67. On the punishment for treason in England, see J. H. Baker, "Criminal Courts and Procedure at Common Law 1550–1800," in *Crime in England, 1550–1800*, ed. J. S. Cockburn (London: Methuen, 1977), p. 42. On the bill of attainder supported by Thomas Jefferson, see Jack Lynch, "A Patriot, a Traitor, and a Bill of Attainder," *Colonial Williamsburg: The Journal of the Colonial Williamsburg Foundation* 24, no. 1 (2002): 12–17, and William Romaine Tyree, "The Case of Josiah Phillips: How Virginia Came to Pass a Bill of Attainder," *Virginia Law Register* 16, no. 9 (1910): 648–58. The Supreme Court cases discussed are as follows: Fletcher v. Peck, 10 U.S. 87 (1810); Cummings v. Missouri, 71 U.S. 277 (1867); Ex parte Garland, 71 U.S. 333 (1867); United States v. Lovett, 328 U.S. 303 (1946); United States v. Brown, 381 U.S. 437 (1965); Selective Service System v. Minnesota Public Interest Research Group, 468 U.S. 841 (1984); Nixon v. Administrator of General Services, 433 U.S. 425 (1977). Quotes from Madison and Hamilton cited in U.S. v. Brown. The case invalidating Amendment 2 is Romer v. Evans, 517 U.S. 620 (1996). The citation for Amar's article is *Michigan Law Review* 95, no. 1 (1996): 203–35. Rick Hills's response is Roderick M. Hills Jr., "Is Amendment 2 *Really* a Bill of Attainder? Some Questions about Professor Amar's Analysis of *Romer*," *Michigan Law Review* 95, no. 1 (1996): 236–54. The Nebraska case is Citizens for Equal Protection v. Bruning, 368 F. Supp. 2d 980 (D. Neb. 2005), *reversed by* 455 F.3d 859 (8th Cir. 2006). Grassley quote: Martin Kady II, "Grassley on AIG Execs: Quit or Suicide," *Politico*, March 16, 2009, http://www.politico.com/news/stories/0309/20083.html. On whether the AIG tax would have been constitutional, see Richard A. Epstein, "Is the Bonus Tax Unconstitutional?" *Wall Street Journal*, March 26, 2009, and Jonathan Adler, "More on AIG Bonus Tax as Bill of Attainder," *Volokh Conspiracy*, March 22, 2009, http://www.volokh.com/posts/1237734930.shtml. The ACORN case in the Second Circuit is ACORN v. United States, 618 F.3d 125 (2nd Cir. 2010). "Somebody has to" and other quotes in that paragraph: ACORN v. United States, 662 F. Supp. 2d 285, 296 (E.D. N.Y. 2009).

CHAPTER 10: THE THIRD AMENDMENT

Peggy Noonan's piece is called "Expect the Unexpected: Why the Third Amendment May Once Again Be Needed," December 7, 2000, available at www.peggynoonan.com/article.php?article=85. The privacy cases I discuss are Griswold v. Connecticut, 381 U.S. 479 (1965); Eisenstadt v. Baird, 405 U.S. 438 (1972); Roe v. Wade, 410 U.S. 113 (1973); and Lawrence v. Texas, 539 U.S. 558 (2003). On substantive due process during the *Lochner* era, see Lochner v. New York, 198 U.S. 45 (1905), and West Coast Hotel Company v. Parrish, 300 U.S. 379 (1937). For a terrific account of FDR's Court-packing plan, see Jeff Shesol, *Supreme Power: Franklin Roosevelt vs. the Supreme Court* (New York: Norton, 2010). On Justice McReynolds being a bigot, see Shesol's book at p. 102, where Shesol describes how McReynolds refused to talk to the Court's two Jewish justices at the time—Justices Brandeis and Cardozo. On Justice Ginsburg and *Roe*, see Linda Greenhouse, "Judge Ginsburg Still Voices Strong Doubts on Rationale Behind Roe v. Wade Ruling," *New York Times*, November 29, 2005. On Ely and *Roe*, see John Hart Ely, "The Wages of Crying Wolf: A Comment on *Roe v. Wade*," *Yale Law Journal* 82, no. 5 (1973): 920–49. On the history of the Third Amendment, the best account (and the one I discuss explicitly in the text) is probably Tom W. Bell, "The Third Amendment: Forgotten but Not Gone," *William & Mary Bill of Rights Journal* 2, no. 1 (1993): 117–50. Other accounts include William S. Fields and David T. Hardy, "The Third Amendment and the Issue of the Maintenance of Standing Armies: A Legal History," *American Journal of Legal History* 35, no. 4 (1991): 393–431; and Seymour W. Wurfel, "Quartering of Troops: The Unlitigated Third Amendment," *Tennessee Law Review* 21, no. 7 (1949): 723–37. The absurd cases I discuss are Custer County Action Association v. Garvey, 256 F.3d 1024 (10th Cir. 2001) (airspace); Jones v. Secretary of Defense, 346 F. Supp. 97 (D. Minn. 1972) (parade); Securities Investor Protection Corporation v. Executive Securities Corporation, 433 F. Supp. 470 (S.D. N.Y. 1977) (subpoena); United States v. Valenzuela, 95 F. Supp. 363 (S.D. Cal. 1951) (Housing and Rent Act). The case from New York involving the National Guard and the correction officer barracks is Engblom v. Carey, 677 F.2d 957 (2nd Cir. 1982). The case on remand in which the lower court held that the officers had "qualified immunity" from money damages was Engblom v. Carey, 572 F. Supp. 44 (S.D. N.Y. 1983). Morton Horwitz's article is "Is the Third Amendment Obsolete?" *Valparaiso University Law Review* 26, no. 1 (1991): 209–14. The ACLU cartoon can be found at www .aclu.org/standup/comics/readbook.php?comicid=14. A picture of the "Repeal the Third Amendment" sign can be found here: www .flickr.com/photos/gemstone/5133666734/. The *Onion* article can be found at www.theonion.com/articles/third-amendment-rights-group-celebrates-another-su,2296/. The articles about creative arguments to revive the Third Amendment are Geoffrey M. Wyatt, "The Third Amendment in the Twenty-first Century: Military Recruiting on Private Campuses," *New England Law Review* 40, no. 1 (Fall 2005): 113–64; Josh Dugan, "When Is a Search Not a Search? When It's a Quarter: The Third Amendment, Originalism, and NSA Wiretapping," *Georgetown Law Journal* 97, no. 2 (2008): 555–87; and Andrew P. Morriss and Richard L. Stroup, "Quartering Species: The 'Living Constitution,' the Third Amendment, and the Endangered Species Act," *Environmental Law* 30 (Fall 2000): 769–810. The quote that ends the chapter is from Mikulski v. Centerior Energy Corporation, 501 F.3d 555, 576 (6th Cir. 2007) (Daughtrey, J., dissenting).

Index